sintimacy

sintimacy

Brian C. johnson

SINTIMACY

Published by Revival Nation Publishing

ISBN 978-1-926625-30-0

Printed in the United States of America

P.O. Box 30001
RPO Eastland Plaza
Sarnia, Ontario
N7T 0A7

www.RevivalNationPublishing.com

Acknowledgements and Dedications

I have to thank many people for their support and encouragement during the writing of *Sintimacy*. This is an intensely personal book and because of the transparency of my own testimony, I must acknowledge my wife Darlene, who has stood with me as I "put our business out in the street" so that others can find freedom. My mistakes became hers, my foibles her embarrassment. Our threefold cord with God has, however, gotten stronger, and because of her formidable character, we both have weathered this storm. Thank you for loving me and standing with me!

Pastors James and Jilline Bond, I am grateful you loved me enough not to throw me away, but to help me realize God's forgiveness and to give me the voice to speak freely in hopes of rescuing others.

Brian Johnson

To Charles and Andy and the other men who came together on Thursday nights at Canalview; I have never known friendship like yours. Thank you for pushing me to be a better husband, father and man of God. My own freedom began because of my ability to be open with all of you.

I am indebted to the members of the Tuesday Writers' Accountability group. Keep writing! Your labors of love are for His Kingdom and shall usher many readers to the heart of the Almighty.

My sincere thanks to Greg Holmes and the great folks at Revival Nation Publishing for being the instruments and vehicles for this book getting to those who need it.

There are so many others, including my good friend Boe Kline, who has helped this book come to life.

This book is dedicated to all of you!

contents

Introduction

How do I tell them? What will they say? How will they react?

These were just some of the thoughts that raced through my head as I stood before my congregation—preparing to tell them my deepest, darkest secret. As a preacher who regularly uses personal stories and interactive exercises, I had asked for those members of the congregation who had been delivered from past addictions to join me at the front of the church. At least 25 people flanked the stage around me. My scripture text for that morning was Hebrews 12:1.

"Wherefore seeing we also are compassed about with so great a cloud of witnesses, let us lay aside every weight, and the sin which doth so easily beset us, and let us run with patience the race that is set before us."

I had two central points to the message: the importance of learning from the mistakes of others and that discipleship includes accountability in relationships. There I was, surrounded by people who were unashamed to say they were a part of "the cloud" and yet, there I was, quivering, a rare response for someone who makes a living by speaking in front of crowds.

Besides, my point had already been made; I had 25 powerful examples—testimonies of deliverance from alcohol, crack cocaine, heroin, and prescription drug addictions. This congregation did not need to hear that one of their ministers had suffered from a serious pornography addiction. They didn't need to know that, at times, I would leave the pulpit and spend hours surfing the dark side of the Internet. They already had enough of the national scandals featuring prominent ministers who had very public falls from grace. They certainly did not need an example this close to home. This would just kill them. I imagined the faces of those young adults whom I had been mentoring. How could I hurt them by exposing my shame? *If they only knew what I was really like, what I struggle with every day, the kinds of thoughts I entertained this week...* How could I reveal a 20-year history of secret addiction, admit a past filled with weaknesses and shame?

Like me, Moses had a past. If you think about it, his is a colorful story. Born under a death sentence, he was abandoned by his mother, who packed him up in a basket and sent him down the river. In what could be called a stroke of good fortune, a princess of Egypt just happened to be bathing in the river and pulled him out. Though raised to be in the lineage of the Pharaoh, it was all taken away in an instant. You know the story: Moses saw one of the Hebrew slaves being mistreated by an overseer and killed the taskmaster. An abandoned baby turned prince of Egypt became a murderer.

Moses ran away in shame. I am not sure why. As prince, he probably could have exonerated himself or at least justified the killing, but he tucked his tail and ran to the backside of a mountain. There he tended sheep for 40 years. The life of a shepherd was a lonely one, with plenty of time to rehearse the mistakes of his past. I can imagine moments of paranoia as he speculated that soldiers would appear at any moment to drag him back to face his crimes. I can just see him nervously looking over his shoulder the first couple of years. I know what that's like—having a secret habit like I did teaches you a thing or two about the fear of getting caught.

Perhaps on a cold night, Moses had a moment to reflect on his past. Perhaps he wondered how he got where he was. "I was a prince, an heir to the throne of Egypt. What am I doing out here sleeping next to a pile of sheep dung?" Imagine—an abandoned baby who became a future king who became a fugitive murderer who became a ragged shepherd on the backside of a mountain. Oh, how many times I sat at that computer and felt like a total failure! How many times I made the promise that I would never do it again, if He would forgive me just one last time!

It was there on that mountain where Moses had an encounter with God. A bush was calling him to a greater purpose than simply facing his own failures. And there I was at my burning bush—standing in front of the congregation. I had exhorted them with James 5:16, *"Confess your faults one to another, and pray for one another, that ye may be healed..."* Each one of those folks who stood near me on the platform had, *"overcome by the blood of the lamb and the word of their testimony"* (Revelation 12:11). And there I was listening to the voice of the Lord telling me, like Moses, to essentially go back to the place of my greatest failure.

The Almighty spoke to Moses about His concern for the children of Israel because of their bonds. It was strange enough to be talking to a bush that actually talked back, but in that moment, when God was saying He was ready to make His big move. I can imagine Moses' life flashed before his eyes. He responded just like I did. In verse 11, Moses basically said, "You want me to do what? Me? You know my story: abandoned baby, prince of a foreign nation, cold-blooded killer on the lamb (no pun intended), old shepherd hiding out on a hill in the middle of a desert. Are you sure you want *me*?"

So, I did it. Standing there, I explained to 200 people that for years I had been hiding my problem. I named it: *pornography*. I tried not to make eye contact with anyone because I anticipated their looks of disappointment. I fully expected the senior pastor would not-so-politely pull me off the platform and scourge me right there in front of everyone. Those elderly grandmas who always told me how much love they had for me…I knew they were clutching their pearls in shocked disgust.

I finished the sermon in tears. I sat down in my usual seat with my head down. I watched as the pastor took his place behind the rostrum, and I prepared for the worst. Instead, he thanked me for my honesty and wrapped his arms around me. He encouraged the congregation to hear the message of accountability as an essential tool in our journey towards spiritual victory.

No one treated me unkindly; the grandmas still loved on me. At least 50 people hugged me afterwards and thanked me for sharing my story. Some of them admitted similar struggles. For the next few weeks, my voicemail and e-mail boxes were full of messages from people who shared how much they wanted to be freed from their own personal chains. Out of all this grew accountability groups; my own freedom from bondage; a Bible study series that ultimately became the book you are reading; and a spirit of transparency that is so needed in the church today.

Later in His encounter with Moses, God asked him an important question. *"What is that in thine hand?"* (Exodus 4:2). It was the tool of a shepherd, the shepherd who bore the stain of past failures. It was that very tool

God would use to show His great power and deliver a people. So there he was—abandoned baby turned prince turned fugitive murderer turned shepherd on the backside of a mountain—who would become the savior of a people because he dared to have his past transformed by an amazing God. This book is my attempt to answer the Lord's question and to follow in Moses' footsteps. My rod is my story of freedom. I am using it to free you and your loved ones.

If you're reading this book, you probably fall into one of three categories:

1. You, yourself, have been struggling with—and hopefully want to break free from—some type of secret sin.
2. You know someone who is struggling with secret sin, but they don't know you know.
3. You are amazed and equally appalled by the sheer number of Christian leaders who are embroiled in some national or local scandal dealing with some type of secret sin and you've felt all the related grief, denial, anger, and depression.

If you are one of these people and you are looking for an answer to the ever-present question "Why?" then keep reading. If none of these categories fits you, keep reading anyway because you will undoubtedly encounter someone who will need you to stand in the gap for them as they break free from the bondage of sin.

Sin is the dreaded beast that haunts every Christian who endeavors to do the will of the Lord. Its influence has plagued each of us, literally since the dawn of time. Adam and Eve had barely walked the breadth of the Garden of Eden before they fell into the grasp of sin. Though eons have passed since that fateful day, each of us bears the mark of the curse of Adam's sin and must daily wage war against its pursuit of total domination of our spiritual lives.

If we're honest, we've all fallen under sin's spell at times. Some battles we win; others are heinous massacres. You can probably recount examples of each: the times you stood your ground and made a strong offensive and the times you were utterly routed and forced to retreat. Hopefully, the victories have been more common than the defeats. This book, however, is not about single struggles. This book is about engaging in the battle of all battles and winning the war against prevailing secret sin. This type of sin is all-consuming and has the power to ruin our lives: personally, professionally, and spiritually.

Pornography, drugs (narcotics, over-the-counter, and prescription), illicit and deviant sexual behavior are just a few of the ways in which some members of the body of Christ have been enslaved to sin. We have become a society given over to its own predilections. Committing sin seems so easy to us, especially since the advent of the Internet. All one has to do is punch a few keys, and they can have the world and all of its sinful pleasures within moments. We no longer have to contend with going to the house of ill repute—the crack house or the whorehouse—to get our "fix." What a shame; it was the going that kept many of us out of those places. It was the fear of someone seeing us and asking, "Hey, I thought you were a Christian. What are you doing here?" That was enough to keep us on the straight-and-narrow. Not so anymore. You can have what you want and do what you want and never leave your house. You can have your sin mail-ordered, and nobody has to know. Just a reminder, *"The eyes of the Lord are in every place, beholding the evil and the good"* (Proverbs 15:3).

Secrecy has caused this proliferation of Christian debauchery. As long as it is hidden, we think we are able to get away with it and we feel justified because "it's not hurting anyone but me." At the heart of this secrecy, though, is the spiritual competition that we seem to have with other Christians. While none of us wants to portray a holier-than-thou attitude, that's exactly how we operate in modern-day Christianity. We all want to appear holy and righteous before others, the operative word being "appear." For many of us, our spiritual lives are mere facades that have been fabricated through attention to the superficial details of clothing, language (churchy talk), church attendance and participation. All the while, we live and die in secret darkness. We live according to a misleading question: "How much sin can I get away with and still make it to heaven?"

If you've been dying in the darkness of secret sin, there is just one way out. The Scriptures dictate the process by which we can be freed. The psalmist asked and answered an important question: *"Wherewithal shall a young man cleanse his way? By taking heed thereto according to thy word"* (119:9). Unlike many other books and workbooks on dealing with sin, this book will stipulate that freedom only occurs with compliance and obedience to the Word of God. No simple force of willpower—although we will emphasize personal responsibility—no simple steps to walk through, and no magic bullets here. Strict adherence to the Word of God, following His Spirit and direction, is the only clear path to true freedom in Christ. This book is not designed to be a theoretical model. I am not here just to explain this concept. I want you, or the one you love, to be freed from *sintimate* behaviors and lifestyles, to be the overcomer that scripture declares we are. The following principles will serve as a rubric for this emancipation process:

1. Pray constantly for deliverance, not just at the time of weakness (Matthew 6:13).
2. Do not neglect the Word of God (Psalm 119:9).
3. Be on the alert concerning temptations and satan's schemes (Ephesians 6:11).
4. Resist satan with spiritual warfare (Ephesians 6:10-18; 1 Peter 5:8-9; Isaiah 58:6).
5. Turn from wickedness and sin (2 Chronicles 7:14).

Please note that this book is written from the perspective of someone who has, "been there, done that, and bought the T-shirt." I am going to be very transparent about my own struggles and how, through vigilant obedience to God's Word, I have found my freedom. Bless God!

Chapter One
What Is Sintimacy?

As a child of the 1970s, I grew up watching shows like *Sesame Street, Mister Rogers' Neighborhood, Zoom, Captain Kangaroo,* and *Romper Room.* These were educational programs on public television. One of my favorites was *The Electric Company* starring acclaimed actors such as Morgan Freeman, Mel Brooks, and Rita Moreno. On each episode, there was a phonics lesson. Two silhouettes would pronounce a word by its sounds. The shadowy figures would face each other; one would say the first sound and the other the second. They would then pronounce the whole word together. For example: "b…at…bat" or "c…at…cat." That's how I came up with the term "*sintimacy.*" The word is made by compounding the words sin and intimacy. Let's take some time to explain both of these terms.

What is Sin?

Sin's most basic definition is missing the mark of righteousness that God sets for His people. Scriptures declare that our footsteps are ordered by God (Psalm 37:23), and He expects us to follow the Spirit. Any time we step outside of those [b]orders, it is sin. To follow our fleshly desires is sin. In archery, the goal is to hit the bulls-eye at the center of the target. Such is our directive from God—walk in the center of My will. Unfortunately, many Christians prefer to walk on, or are satisfied with, the periphery of righteousness. They often live with the thought "How much sin can I get away with and still make it to heaven?" Many would argue they are not making this decision consciously. The rules of geometry dictate that the shortest distance between two points is a straight line. Hmm, how might this be true in the rules of holy living?

Sin, at various times throughout scripture, is also denoted as transgression, wrongdoing, wickedness, injustice, failure to love (think about that one), defiance of the law of God, and finally, an enslaving and deceiving power. It is this last one that we will spend a great deal of time discussing. From these definitions, we can conclude that the essence of sin is selfishness—a grasping of things or pleasures for ourselves, regardless of the welfare of others and the commandments of God. Ultimately, sin becomes the refusal to be subject to God and His Word. In his text, *Not the Way It's Supposed to Be: A Breviary of Sin* (1995), author Neal Plantinga describes sin in this manner:

> *"It is finally unknown, irrational, alien. Sin is always a departure from the norm and is assessed accordingly. Sin is deviant and perverse, an injustice, inequity, or ingratitude. Sin in the Exodus literature is disorder and disobedience [sic]. Sin is faithlessness, lawlessness, godlessness. Sin is both the overstepping of a line and the failure to reach it—both transgression and shortcoming.*

> *Sin is a missing of the mark, a spoiling of the goods, a staining of garments, a hitch in one's gait, a wandering from the path, a fragmenting of the whole. Sin is what culpably disturbs shalom. Sinful human life is a caricature of proper human life." (p. 88)*

Giving in to the power of sin, for the Christian, is supposed to be a non-issue. Numerous scriptures indicate that once we come to Christ, we have power over sin; are dead to sin; have been raised to new life; and are no longer servants to sin. Yet, everywhere we turn, Christians are falling under its spell. I've deduced that the main reason is that we make excuses so we can do whatever we want. There are many excuses for giving in to sin. Three of the most popular are "I'm only human," "The devil made me do it," and "Nobody's perfect." Most of the excuses we give are meant to shift the blame and responsibility to someone other than "me." The problem with these excuses is that the Bible contradicts them all. God has made us new, old things are passed away; we have been given authority and power to resist the devil; and through His strength, we are made perfect. The reality is, however, that Christians have lost sight of the target, the "mark for the prize of the *high* calling of God," (Philippians 3:14) and at the same time, have confused God's grace and mercy for weakness, blindness, or stupidity. What we forget is God's high expectations for righteousness. We have, in many ways, forgotten the biblical examples of failure and its consequences.

Remember the story of Adam and Eve? God's handmade creations were given the entire Garden of Eden to govern and in a split second, lost it all for simply eating a piece of fruit. Moses, the only person to have a face-to-face meeting with God, was forbidden to enter the land of promise because he hit a rock with a stick. Unlike Moses, King Saul did not kill someone, yet he and his descendants lost the kingdom forever. These individual acts of disobedience brought God's wrath. How do you think He feels about

His children who continually live in secret sin?

Our natural, fleshly inclination is to hide our sins. Both Adam and his son Cain had secret sins. Adam, in his shame, sewed fig leaves together to hide his nakedness. When the Lord found him and Eve, they were hiding among the trees in the Garden. This is the problem of living in sin. The shame and guilt cause us to shun God. We are afraid and uncomfortable in His presence, rightfully fearful of His glory. When we are in sin, we feel it is impossible to draw near to Him with confidence. We run from Him, instead of to Him for deliverance. Like Adam and Eve, our sinful conditions cause us to retreat from the presence of God, despite the scriptural urging to, *"boldly approach the throne of grace, that we may obtain mercy"* (Hebrews 4:16). This avoidance of God is coupled with a willful isolation from others within our faith communities. We just do not want people to know how we have failed. Most churches operate in a punitive manner that has zero tolerance for those who lead habitually sinful lives.

Cain murdered his brother Abel and buried his body. When confronted by God, Cain did what most of us do—he acted like he didn't know it was wrong. He pretended he hadn't seen Abel. Christians do this quite well. They say, "It was just a mistake. I couldn't help it. It was someone else's fault. I was pressured into doing it. Everyone's doing it." These phrases are used to cover up our own culpability or to shift blame, but as noted inventor George Washington Carver once argued, "Ninety-nine percent of all failures come from people who have the habit of making excuses."[1] God cursed Cain for his hidden sin and instead of responding with repentance, Cain separated himself from God and decided to live as a fugitive and a vagabond (Genesis 4:14). There is a danger in unrepentant sin and the hubris it creates in our hearts.

What continues to be problematic is the confusion or misuse of the idea of God's grace and mercy. Contemporary Christians have, as a fellow minister calls it, a "*greasy grace philosophy.*" We typically speak of grace only as it relates to the expectation of blessing: God's unmerited favor. Grace is much, much more than that. God's revelation of grace is what gives us the ability to act righteously. It is an enabling power to do what is right, not an excuse to commit sin at will. You should consider grace an entryway into the will of God. Mercy, on the other hand, is protection from God's wrath. It is the unmerited grace to receive a buy when we really deserve punishment. More than others, parents probably understand the concept of mercy. If our children only knew how many times we let them off the hook!

"[Grace] is an enabling power to do what is right, not an excuse to commit sin at will."

Isn't it interesting that we intrinsically know how to do wrong before we know how to do right? One of the first things a toddler learns to do is tell a lie. Have you ever asked a young child if they took the cookie or drew on the wall with the crayon? When asked, they automatically say "no" or "I don't know." This is proof of a natural predisposition and connection to the father of lies (John 8:44). Because of the mark of sin on our lives, we make inherently bad decisions; hence, the necessity of being ordered by the Lord (Psalm 37:23) and being transformed by the renewing of our mind (Romans 12:2).

We must remember that our sin is against God and God alone—no matter whom it is with or what the activity is. In his prayer of repentance in Psalm 51, King David recognized the stain of sin, a sort of birth defect. Despite this congenital disorder, his ultimate allegiance was to the purity of God's holiness.

Joseph held a similar standard. In the Genesis account, Joseph had been appointed caretaker of Potiphar's house. Potiphar was a member of the personal staff of the pharaoh and served as the captain of the palace guard. He entrusted his household to Joseph. Potiphar's wife was enamored by the strapping young lad and set a plan in place to have sexual relations with him. In his rejection of her advances, Joseph proclaimed that not only did he not want to disrespect his master, Potiphar, but he asked, *"How could I ever do such a wicked thing? It would be a great sin against God"* (Genesis 39:9).

What is Intimacy?

"Be ye therefore followers of God, as dear children; and walk in love, as Christ also hath loved us, and hath given himself for us an offering and a sacrifice to God for a sweet-smelling savor" (Ephesians 5:1-2).

The above scripture speaks to how we *walk in love* with Christ. (It is important to note that when scripture uses the word walk or stand it refers to a continual journey [cf. Psalm 24:3]. *"Who shall ascend into the hill of the Lord, and who shall stand in his holy place?"* To exemplify walking in love, I asked members of our church who had been married for 50, 40, 30, 20, and 10 years to answer the following two questions:

1) How did you know you were in love with your spouse? and
2) How did you know your partner loved you?

You can probably anticipate their responses. Those who had been married for longer periods of time referenced love and intimacy as surviving tough times, commitment to see one another through difficult situations, a deep friendship and a constancy of caring—all developed from a mutual admiration, respect and care for the other. The younger lovers tended to speak about physical feelings. One used the term "getting the woo-hoos" (goose bumps and a fluttering stomach) when the other person walked into the room. They spoke of the language of looking at one another and being drawn to them. Both groups described a sense of longing for the other, an internal hunger of sorts where they felt that part of them was missing when the other was not around. Their intimacy was described as a completeness only made possible by walking together in love.

What is revealed in these descriptions is the very personal nature of long-term intimate relationships. One of the respondents indicated to me that intimacy is best described as a "face-to-face, heart-to-heart, and soul-to-soul connection." Another stated, "Intimacy is about completely giving yourself over to someone." One used the term "soul deepness," which indicated an intense connection between the couples. Still another described intimacy as a willingness to make yourself vulnerable with another person, someone who you are so comfortable with that you can truly be yourself—unmasked. In his book *Intimacy: A 100 Day Guide to Better Relationships*, Dr. Doug Weiss, executive director of Heart to Heart Counseling Centers, describes intimacy as a process whereby two persons come to a oneness that is not derived from accidental coincidence.

Intimacy is exclusionary. It is private and shared only with an extremely limited number of people. Even though human beings are drawn to communal experiences and friendships, we choose to be intimate only with those who share a similar affinity and attraction. Even if our list of friends is rather lengthy, we may never come to levels of personal intimacy with many of them. People who share intimacy are often able to communicate on a different wavelength than others. My wife and I are frequently accused of being able to just look at each other and know what the other is thinking. Often we finish each other's statements or start singing a song that was only playing in the mind of the other! We are often most comfortable with our intimate partners. We are able to relax and *let it all hang out*. We are very protective of our intimacies, and we relish in the ability to keep private matters private. What is even better about intimacy is that it is a shared experience between persons who care about each other and who are interested in mutual success and reward. The couple shares a firm commitment to each other, and they are on a journey together towards a common purpose—a mind, body, and spirit connection.

What we must grasp is that intimacy is not only incredibly personal, but it is also incredibly possessive. Possessive in the sense that we "own" folks whom we are intimate with. Think about *my* wife or *my* husband. As in physical intimacy, we carry, and pass on, remnants of every sexual relationship we have ever had with someone. Possessive in the sense that we become submissive to our intimate partner, willing to do whatever pleases the other person. When married couples are physically intimate, they become willing to do whatever pleases the other—for the most part. It is the closeness of intimacy that drives us to do this. When we are so completely rapt with love and desire for our partner, it becomes our mission to perform in ways that ensure our inti*MATE* is pleased.

◇◇

"Intimacy is not only incredibly personal, but it is also incredibly possessive."

◇◇

A lifestyle of sin is no different; it becomes very possessive and reluctant to let us go. Sin seeks ownership and dominion over us to the point where we are willing and submissive to its call and desire. We become driven to please these lusts and desires to the extent that we will try almost anything in order to please the sinful nature.

For most of us, intimacy is a sexually charged term. It is the moments of closeness we share with a precious loved one when we are naked and unashamed. Every flaw and imperfection is on display, but typically we don't worry about it because the other person cares deeply for us. A similar sexual word is desire. Let's look at this word that is made up of two syllables, "de" and "sire." The prefix "de" means "from" or "to" and is a possessive term. "Sire" is a title of authority such as for a king, and it is also the term used when a male horse mounts and impregnates a female. For the sinful, desire is no different. Your sin is either taking authority in your life or it is mounting you, figuratively speaking, and planting seeds for future destruction.

What is Sintimacy?

When I first starting teaching on this subject, I asked adult and youth members of my congregation to define the words sin and intimacy and then combine their definitions to create the meaning of *sintimacy*. Some of their responses are in the following table:

Sin	**+ Intimacy**	**= Sintimacy**
Something that goes against God's character	Closeness, Love	The love for anything that goes against God's character
Opposite of what God expects of us	Passionate sequences	Sinning passionately
Anything out of line with the will of God	Living in communion with God and others; soul deepness (mind, body, and spirit)	Willfully living out of line of the will of God and choosing to live in communion with sin

Transgression of the Word of God	The ultimate showing or giving of love between each other	The ultimate transgression
Anything that's not right unto God	Something you love that you would not separate from	Loving doing wrong so much that you can't separate yourself from it
Bad things you do (wickedness, lying, cheating stealing, etc); not letting go	Love someone; getting close to God; soul-to-soul connection; my will and God's will	When there is no separation between the bad things you do and your soul connection
That which separates us from God	Being as close as you can get with God or with your loved ones	The sin that we keep so close to ourselves that we don't show anyone and we think we can hide from God
Any act of disobedience to God	A deep crossing of emotions, spirit, and mind	A deep crossing of emotions that is disobedient to God
Disobeying God and His Word	Giving yourself to another in love	Doing the wrong thing; giving yourself over to disobedience
To fall short of; to commit to wrongdoing	To find your most innermost feelings of love and compassion	Justification to think my will is God's will

Conscious decision to do something morally, ethically, or theologically incorrect; pleasing yourself at the cost of something or someone else	Deep selfless love of loyalty and commitment	A love of self; conscious, willful decision of relationship to a thing or person that costs you morally, ethically, spiritually, physically
Doing something wrong; wrongdoing; not obeying God	An internal relationship with someone or God; someone knowing your innermost desires	An internal desire to do something wrong
Doing what God commands not be done	The private lives between a husband and a wife	Privately doing what God commands us not to
Anything contrary to God's Word	To give yourself completely to another person	To give yourself completely to being contrary to God's Word
Disobedience to the Word and will of God	Relationship with no barriers	Relationship with the world with no barriers; nothing will stop me from being disobedient to the Word of God
Anything that goes against God's Word	Sharing things that are personal and secret	Personal things that you would like to keep secret from God

Sin is lying, cheating, stealing; all these things don't please God	Share in secret thoughts with friends	Stealing, lying, and cheating and telling your friends but asking them to keep quiet
Things that are wrong that Christians should not engage themselves in; going against the will of God	A close relationship with someone or something you love	Things that you love or have a close relationship with and are engaged in that are wrong and unacceptable to God
An action that causes you to do wrong	Being deeply involved with something	Being deeply involved with things that cause you to do wrong
Something you do that you shouldn't do and you know it's wrong	A sexual relationship with another person	Something, like sex, that you do that you know is wrong and you do it over and over until it's a part of you

The previous chart reveals the nature of a *sintimate* lifestyle, where the selfish desires of our human nature take precedence over the Word and will of God for our lives. There is a soul deepness where our carnality is superimposed upon our spirituality. It must be stated that spiritual death by sinful behavior is a process of the choices we make. The chart describes willful, conscious acts of disobedience against the will, authority, purpose, plan and power of God. The comments describe a love for the grey area where holiness and iniquity blend into some indistinguishable slush. They reference a giving up, or a giving in, or giving ourselves over to be ruled by hidden sin—and delighting in it. In the book of Deuteronomy, chapter 30, Moses instructed that, each day there is the choice between prosperity and disaster, blessings and cursing, and life and death. He also wisely stated that keeping God's commandments is preservative for our lives and those of our lineage. Elsewhere, he cautioned that the consequences of sin can visit the third or fourth generation. In the end, the question remains, "Do we love God more than our own pleasure?"

Ted Haggard, defrocked leader of the *National Evangelical Association*, revealed the dangers of living *sintimately*. In the sermon "*Living as if There are No Secrets*," Haggard stated, "Sin will take you farther than you want to go. It will cost you more than you want to pay. It will keep you longer than you want to stay." Haggard's oddly prophetic comments were given approximately two years before his own *sintimacy* was revealed. They indicate the spiritual tug-of-war that operates in our lives. Sadly, the carnal pull is dragging many Christians to the wrong side, partly because it is much easier to do wrong than to do right. God's expectations are high—but not unattainable—and the *sintimate* prefer comfortably lower standards.

We must recognize that our level of intimacy with things that are ungodly greatly impacts our ability to live a holy, separated, and sanctified life. *Sintimacy* retards holy living; it makes it lame; it makes it weak; it saps the strength; and it saps the power. We walk around with no power against satan. We are unable to command him to move out of our way because we have been consorting for too long with the enemy.

In their comments above, the couples I interviewed described intimacy as a process that happens over time and through some struggle. Dr. Doug Weiss argues that honesty and openness are crucial to intimacy. *Sintimacy*, however, operates on the exact opposite path, in secrecy and shame. In the

1970s, there was a song that revealed the very nature of shame: low down and dirty. Shame is a painful emotion caused by consciousness of guilt, shortcoming or impropriety. The *sintimate* become far too acquainted with this paralyzing shame. They become one with the sinful condition, seeing themselves only as failures rather than the recipients of God's enabling grace and purifying mercy.

As mentioned above, *sintimacy* is a progressive disorder that has a number of symptoms, behaviors, and attributes. Below, I want to offer a list of these attributes:

- **Looking over our shoulder.** Let's face facts. If we have to look over our shoulder wondering who's watching, then we should probably not be doing whatever it is we are getting ready to do.
- **Rationalizing one sin—that becomes two…** Whenever we justify our wrongdoing, it makes it so much easier to do again and again.
- **Having difficultly distinguishing between what is godly and what isn't.** The *sintimate* can justify self by thinking their will is God's will. Furthermore, they learn to expect God's blessing despite their lifestyle of sin. When we blur the line between what is God and what is not, when we cannot distinguish between what is holy and what isn't, there's a problem. Too many Christians like the blur.
- **Acting like nothing is wrong.** The denial of secret sin makes us put on a nice, religious façade. We wear the "right" clothes and talk the "right" talk, go on with our usual duties (preaching, teaching, witnessing, etc.), and go on our merry ways. Paul referenced the *sintimate* in 2 Timothy 3:5, when he stated, *"They will act as if they are religious, but they will reject the power that could make them godly"* (NLT).
- **Getting the "can't-help-its."** The can't-help-its are killing

Christians. What we must acknowledge, however, is that we make the cross ineffective when we say we can't help ourselves when it comes to sin.

- **Relegating godly responsibilities to second or third place—or allowing them to become a chore.** Christianity, for many, has become a chore. It's a bother to pray. We're too busy to read God's Word. People don't even want to go to church anymore. A word of caution: If doing the things that bring us closer to God is a bother, then there is a major problem in our spiritual relationship with the Lord. Isn't it interesting that we always have time to fulfill the lusts of the flesh?
- **Becoming a wanderer.** Wanderers are those who seem to have no direction. They often continue going in circles, searching for old landmarks, trying to find their rightful place. They often get on what I call the cycle of sin (you know it: sin, "Lord forgive me," sin, "Lord forgive me," sin, "Lord forgive me") with no change in behavior. It's like riding a stationary bike. You pedal and pedal but go nowhere. Please do not get me wrong; asking for forgiveness is an essential element, but true repentance means turning from doing the same old things: a transformation of heart, mind, and action.
- **Allowing our conscience to become seared.** There is a conscience-searing that takes place when we repeatedly sin. Searing a piece of meat locks in the juices and locks out everything else. Most good chefs know that, when a steak is fully seared, it will easily release from the pan. Imagine then, for the *sintimate* Christian whose consciousness has been seared by sin, it is easy to be released from God (1 Timothy 4:2).
- **Becoming a dog that returns to his own vomit.** We continue to return to the place of our greatest sickness and failure and expect to have victory. I heard someone mention the definition of insanity as, "doing the same thing over and over again and expecting a

different result."

In Acts 8:18-25, Simon sought to purchase the power of the Spirit that was manifested through Peter. Peter rebuked him by saying the gift was not available to him because his "heart [was] not right in the sight of God." Simon was rejected by God because he was still wicked, entangled in the bond of iniquity. Any supernatural experience thought to be the baptism in the Spirit that occurs in one who continues to follow the sinful ways of the flesh is not of Christ.

At this point, I think it is important for us to see *sintimacy* in action—although you are probably all too aware of what it looks like in your own life. I am going to use a very familiar story to explain how *sintimacy* works. Let's look at the story of *Goldilocks and the Three Bears*. You may imagine this as merely a fictional children's story, but significant spiritual truths emerge as we explore the process of *sintimacy*.

This familiar tale--or at least the version most of us remember--follows a young girl named Goldilocks (so called for her shiny golden locks of hair) who wanders into a wooded area far from home. Hungry and tired, Goldilocks enters the home of a family of bears who had gone on a walk before they would eat their meal of porridge. The young visitor tasted from each of the bowls—one was too hot, one too cold, and one just right, which she promptly devoured. After eating, she nestled in a chair next to the fireplace to catch a few winks of sleep. When her chair broke, she went upstairs to find a comfy bed to sleep in—one was too hard, one too soft, and the other just right. Falling fast to sleep, Goldilocks was unaware that the bears had return to find the clues of her invasion. As she rested, the bears found her; the voice of the smallest bear startled her and she was able to escape the house unscathed. Both Goldilocks and the Bear family were thereafter able to "live happily ever after."

Where did Goldilocks go wrong in her walk? How does her story parallel that of a *sintimate* Christian? Her journey from home and experiences in the wilderness are very telling.

- She entered a strange land.
- She walked deeper into the wilderness.
- She did something she would not ordinarily do.
- She opened the door of a stranger's house.
- She took a good whiff.
- She took a taste.
- She asked, "How much can I get away with?"
- She got the "–itis" (falling asleep after eating).
- She got comfortable in a stranger's house.
- She ignored the wake-up call.
- She went even deeper into the house.
- She fell asleep.

Goldilocks' first problem was being out in the woods alone. For the life of me, I can't figure out why, in all of these types of fairy tales, little girls are out in the wilderness by themselves. The characters in the stories are most often children: *Goldilocks*, *Little Red Riding Hood*, *Hansel and Gretel*, etc. Look at the imagery related to the definition of a wilderness: "an unsettled, uncultivated region left in its natural condition, especially: a) a large wild tract of land covered with dense vegetation or forests; b) an extensive area that is barren or empty; a waste; or, c) a piece of land set aside to grow wild."[2] The wilderness in children's stories is dark, where things go bump in the night; it's where trees eat people and where monsters live. Goldilocks should never have been in a place like this.

If we look at this definition from a biblical/spiritual perspective, the wilderness is not a place for Christians to be hanging out either. The dark place is not the right element for children of light. Light and darkness cannot share the same space.

She was out in the wilderness and recognized she was tired and hungry. Being in the wilderness can do that—make us tired and make us seek things that will meet our needs. Typically, when we are dealing with the issues of *sintimacy*—the tough stuff, temptations and struggles—and we're in the dark place, we begin to seek those things. When we're living in the wilderness, the hunger intensifies, and when the hunger intensifies, the "I gottas" get stronger.

You must understand Goldilocks was from a good home. How do we know this? She had *golden locks*. Think about the pictures you've seen; she is well kempt. In the old stories and movies, the mean and evil people wore black, but not our heroine. She was well-dressed and her hair was beautifully maintained. She had some good "home training," as they say. Doesn't it seem odd that a young girl from a good home is out in the woods by herself?

As she was wandering through the woods, she came upon a house. Maybe it was the only house out there and she realized she was a little too far from home. Nevertheless, she knocked on the door, but no one was home. It seems to me, though, that someone with some home training who knocked on a door and got no response wouldn't just walk in, even *if* the door was open. I am sure that, at some point, Goldilocks' parents told her it was inappropriate to commit break and entry. I wonder how many strange, open-doored houses Christians are walking into. That's the problem of *sintimacy*—when we get out into the wilderness, we do things we would not ordinarily do, even things we have been instructed not to do.

Sintimacy permitted Goldilocks to take the extra step of turning the doorknob to enter the house of a stranger somewhere in the middle of the wilderness. Remember, the stranger was not home; she was entering the home uninvited—maybe just for a peek. Remember, too, that *sintimacy* often operates in secrecy. I guarantee you Goldilocks did not proudly announce her arrival. I imagine she looked over her shoulder a couple of times and tiptoed into the house. She peeked in; she did not just burst through the door. Why? Because she knew she was in the wrong. She was not visiting her friend's house or delivering a picnic basket to Grandma. She was in the woods, breaking into the home of a complete stranger. Friend, if you have to sneak a peek over your shoulder to see who's watching, chances are you are walking into a *sintimate* situation. Chances are the activity is something you are not supposed to be doing.

◇◇

"Sin will take you farther than you want to go. It will cost you more than you want to pay. It will keep you longer than you want to stay."

◇◇

When we live in *sintimacy*, sometimes we get into these quandaries about whether or not something is wrong. If we have to think about it, it's probably better—and safer—to err on the side of caution and not do it. Trust me; it will save you a whole lot of trouble.

Goldilocks got into the house. Outside, there was still a chance to back away. There was a way of escape. Before she entered the strange place, she could have remembered she was out of her element, that she had a home where she could be safe, well-fed, and rested. But remember Ted Haggard's words, *"Sin will take you farther than you want to go. It will cost you more than you want to pay. It will keep you longer than you want to stay."* *Sintimacy* took her into the house, and there she was, alone in the strange place. What happened next? The hunger intensified. You probably understand being in the wilderness and feeling your hunger intensify. Your stomach starts to growl. How you experience the growling may be different, depending on the *sintimacy*, but as your hunger grows, there's a signal that goes off in your brain that requires you to appease that god. We must understand that, when we repeatedly yield to sin's attempts at dominance, we are elevating that thing to the place of authority and sovereignty in our lives because it has control over us.

Do you remember the reason Goldilocks entered the house? She was hungry and in search of food. Surprise, surprise! In the house, she came upon not one bowl of porridge, but three. She picked the right stranger's house to get her need met. The *sintimate* would see this phenomenon as a blessing from the Lord. "I was hungry, and look at that, there's food on the table. He is Jehovah Jireh! God opened this door for me!" Fool, you are out in the wilderness in a strange land; the Lord did not open the door for you and provide the meal.

Sintimacy lulls us into misconstrued thinking that God will justify our position in the dark place because "He's going to use me here." I have heard teens tell me that, even though their friends are hanging out and doing drugs or drinking, it does not necessarily mean they will, too. In fact, they say they're spending time with them to win them to the Lord, being a good Christian witness. If you're shaking your head right now, you probably know this type of thinking is faulty. Do I mean Christians can't handle being around those who smoke and drink or…(you fill in the blank)? Can't we win them there? All I'm saying is that I'm crazy enough to believe, if God wants to save someone who is lost, His Spirit will draw that person out of the house and down the path to where I am so I don't have to go into the wilderness and possibly get trapped. Don't get me wrong; I do believe God will send certain people into the wilderness to go and rescue someone who needs deliverance, but I find it interesting that, in Mark 8, Jesus Himself had to remove a blind man from the cursed place of Bethsaida in order to perform the miracle. So, it seems to me, at times, it is appropriate for a Christian to go—with the Spirit's leading and empowerment—into the dark place, but certainly not to go and hang out. Most likely, though, if you are struggling with a particular sin, the Lord is not going to require you to go to the place of your struggle to win someone. It's a trap. It would be too easy for such a person to go in and get caught in the quicksand. I could make the argument that Jesus called His disciples to be fishermen, not hunters; fishermen use bait and cast a line to draw the fish to them.

Goldilocks stood looking at the bowls of porridge and decided to take a taste. The first bowl was too hot. There are certain activities a Christian will look at and say, "Absolutely not!" That particular action is not tempting at all; it's too hot. But watch how *sintimacy* works. She went to the next bowl, and it was too cold. Again, certain activities are not attractive or tempting. She made one more try and found the bowl of porridge that was just right and sat down for a feast. This is a classic example of what my former pastor, Rev. Eric Brooks, calls "How much sin can I get away with and still make it to heaven?" The *sintimate* will keep trying certain activities, knowing they are wrong until they find one that is either easy to keep hidden or one that is easier to justify.

After eating to her *sintimacy's* content, Goldilocks got very sleepy. My friends call this the "itis," a condition where people start falling asleep soon after a meal. I believe the real medical condition is called reactive hypoglycemia. Immediately after having found the *sintimacy* that was "just right," she got sleepy. Watch how *sintimacy* works. She was in the house of a stranger deep in the wilderness. She ate a tempting meal that, though prepared for someone else, was somehow just right for her. Then, instead of leaving, she went and sat down in a chair next to the fire. Again, she tried out several different chairs looking for the one that was just right. In real estate, they say it's all about location. Goldilocks' just right chair was located next to the fire. This should have been another warning sign. Take note also that each time she found her just right spot, it was in the baby bear's place. Scriptures record it is the "little foxes" that "ruin the vineyard of love" (Song of Solomon 2:15). The *sintimate* often try the little things because they think the little temptations and activities are safe.

While taking her little nap in the comfy chair, the chair breaks, but still that does not wake her up. She preferred to stay comfortably resting in a stranger's house in the dark wilderness, the owners soon to return. A *sintimate* Christian begins to prefer the comfort of the darkness. The broken chair was a sign from the Lord to wake up and take notice of her location. In the story of the prodigal son, the lost boy found himself in a pig sty. The scripture says that "*he came to himself*" (Luke 15:17). In other words, he took stock of his location and realized what his life had become. It was then that he decided to return home—but not our Goldilocks. You would think, after eating someone else's food *and* destroying their property, Goldilocks would get out of the house. *Sintimacy* had her so tired she ignored the wake-up call.

Sintimacy sent her upstairs to lie down. I watch a lot of the crime dramas on TV. Have you ever noticed that, when the criminals are trying to escape the police's grasp, they almost always run upstairs towards the roof? Going deeper into the building is no way to escape. In fact, it almost always ensures their capture and, in extreme cases, a leap to their deaths. *Goldilocks* may be a children's story, but I hope you're catching the spiritual nuggets.

Once upstairs, Goldilocks was met with the same three choices: beds that were too hard, too soft, and just right. She chose the comfy baby bed, and the story tells us she fell dead asleep—so asleep she didn't know the bears had returned and were searching for the person who had entered their territory, eaten their food, and destroyed their property. Watch how your soul's enemy works: He follows your tracks. He likes it when we take his food because, like stray cats, if we take the bait once, it is difficult to get rid of us. The bears found Goldilocks asleep.

Interestingly enough, it was the voice of the baby bear that awakened the sleeping girl. Goldilocks jumped out of the bed and tried to run away from the little bitty bear, but what she didn't realize was that the baby was flanked by two larger bears. We have to understand that, even though we're messing around with the "little baby bears" in our lives, when we get into such a wilderness place, those little ones have some big friends. And now that we've realized we have been in this place—tasting and trying what was "just right" and comfortable for us—there are three hungry bears ready to pounce on the sleeping, *sintimate* Christian.

Note that the bears could have found Goldilocks and said nothing—just started ripping her to shreds. They would have been well within their rights to do so; Goldilocks was in their home, had eaten their food, broken their chair, and was now fast asleep in their private bedroom. The bears' natural instinct would have been to eat her, just as the devil's job is to steal, kill, and destroy (John 10:10). Despite all of this, the grace and mercy of God was in action. Even though she was in the wrong place, had done many of the wrong things, and had fallen spiritually asleep, it was the grace of God that allowed Goldilocks to hear the little bear's voice. Even though she ignored the earlier warning of the broken chair, He awakened her from a deep sleep with a "still, small voice." The mercy of God allowed her to escape the clutches of three angry bears and get out of the house in the wilderness. The grace of God—God's plan of escape—is given long before we get into the wilderness. Often we do not listen and willingly go into the stranger's house to try their wares. Yet, somehow, He allows us to escape judgment and destruction. King David was right: *"His faithful love [mercy] endures forever!"* (Psalm 107:1).

Chapter Two
Secrets, Lies, and Tests

A. Temptations, Trials, and Tests

The book of James spends a great deal of time on the effects of temptation. Described as the source of sin, temptation is often equated with a powerful force that has a great deal of sway in our decision making. James 1:12-16 outlines the process of temptation.

"Blessed is the man that endureth temptation: for when he is tried, he shall receive the crown of life, which the Lord hath promised to them that love him. Let no man say when he is tempted, I am tempted of God: for God cannot be tempted with evil, neither tempteth he any man: But every man is tempted, when he is drawn away of his own lust, and enticed. Then when lust hath conceived, it bringeth forth sin: and sin, when it is finished, bringeth forth death. Do not err, my beloved brethren."

It is important to note that this word, temptation, shows the limitations of the English language; we have only one meaning for it. It is used often in the Scriptures. In English, the word tempt is, however, more than an enticement to sin. There is also an urging to do what it right. Understanding the difference is crucial to winning the battle for righteousness. We must also be aware that there are multiple sources for our enticements.

In the quest to remain pure in our walk with the Lord, we need to understand how temptation works. *Sintimacy* is greatly impacted by the temptations in our life. Famed pastor, Bishop T.D. Jakes, once asserted that all sin and problems in human relationships can be traced to the "lust of the flesh, the lust of the eyes, and the pride of life" (1 John 2:16). The lust of the flesh includes a drawing towards impure desires, sinful pleasures, and sensual gratification. Because many people interpret lust as simply related to sexual pursuits, it is important to note that sensual gratification refers to being preoccupied by and indulging appetites of all kinds—what can be seen, heard, smelled, touched, and tasted (Genesis 3:3; 1 Corinthians 6:18; James 1:14; Philippians 3:19).Yes, sexual lust can be included here, but there are many more enticements of the flesh.

The lust of the eyes refers to coveting or desiring those things that are attractive to the eye but forbidden by God, including the desire to watch that which gives sinful pleasure. Much of what we view and hear in the mass media today is spiritually harmful to us. If we are not careful, it is easy to be sucked in by the world's entertainment featuring pornography, violence, ungodliness, and immorality. Moses' instructions about coveting certainly coincide with this teaching. Desiring what someone else has can quickly lead us astray (Genesis 3:6; Joshua 7:21; 2 Samuel 11:2; Matthew 5:28).

All around us, we face the temptations of the pride of life. This references the spirit of arrogance, pride, and self-sufficient independence that refuses to recognize the sovereignty of Christ and His Word as the final authority.

The human tendency to put self first—to exalt, glorify, and promote selfish desires and pursuits—is uniquely juxtaposed to the nature of God (James 4:16).

Later in this section, we will discuss the biblical truth that temptations are internal, not from some outside source. Satan, however, does use the aforementioned lusts—flesh, eyes, pride of life—as tools to draw the *sintimate*. Let's look at two examples, one from the story of Adam and Eve, the other from Christ's earthly walk.

When the serpent came to Eve, as recorded in the third chapter of Genesis, he used these lusts to his advantage. Eve must have been hungry at the time because his first appeal was to her flesh. God had granted the first couple permission to eat from any tree in the Garden of Eden except one, the tree of the knowledge of good and evil. Perhaps Eve was standing there trying to figure out which of the bountiful blessings she would eat. Maybe her eyes flickered from tree to tree as she tried to make a decision. Capitalizing on Eve's physical hunger, the serpent spoke directly to her sensual lust. "Eat the fruit and you will be satisfied." Secondly, he appealed to the lust of the eyes. Standing there in the midst of the Lord's handmade orchard, the fruit of this particular tree must have had that special "ting" from the toothpaste commercials. The serpent told her to ignore God's promise of death. "You won't die," he said. "In fact, if you eat the fruit, your eyes will be opened. You'll see the world differently; you'll really know what's going on." The scripture indicates that Eve "saw that the tree was good for food, and that it was pleasant to the eyes." Finally, satan delivered the blow that is still being heard around the world. He hit her with the pride of life. "You'll be just like God—knowing all, seeing all—if you just eat the fruit." She succumbed to the desire to make herself wise, to be a know-it-all. In that moment, the idyllic state changed to our present reality. I guess the adage is true: Ignorance is bliss.

When Jesus began His earthly ministry, God commissioned and placed

His seal of approval on Him: *"This is my beloved son, in whom I am well pleased"* (Matthew 3:17). He was then *"led up of the Spirit into the wilderness to be tempted of the devil."* Satan's plan was to get Jesus to deny God's sovereignty and thwart His kingdom plan by appealing to the lusts of the flesh, eyes, and pride of life. This story is chronicled in the fourth chapter of Mark's gospel. Jesus had just completed a 40-day fast, and undoubtedly He was starving. Satan's first appeal was, again, to the physical. He challenged the Christ to turn a stone into bread. He then challenged His ego. *"If you really are the son of God; hurl yourself off this precipice and see if the angels will catch you."* Notice satan's use of scripture to try to mislead Jesus. This was a direct quote of the Old Testament text in Psalms 91:11-12. Be wary of satan's tricks! Thirdly, satan told Jesus to look at the lands surrounding Him. The devil promised to give the kingdoms to Jesus *if* He would just bow down and worship at satan's feet. This one especially angered Jesus because He had His allegiance in the right place. Nothing and no one would take the place of His Father, the Almighty. Would to God that believers would get this singleness of heart!

Eve was deceived, yes, but Adam fell because he loved Eve more than God's Word to him. That's a pretty strong statement, but if you really think about it, you'll see it's true nonetheless. Jesus Himself made a similarly direct statement. *"If you love me, keep my commandments"* (John 14:15). There is no way around it. When a person chooses to commit a sinful act, whether a single act or a continual walk, and refuses to follow God's Word, it is proof that their love allegiance is not with Christ.

Being able to distinguish who is behind the temptation can teach us how to respond in the midst of each circumstance. Knowing the difference can impact our ability to pass. These two examples are indicative of spiritual trials and tests. In this story, Jesus was led into the wilderness to be tempted/tested by the devil. How do we know it was a test? Look at Jesus' response.

Each time He was tempted, He responded with what He knew: the Word. Our children's teachers spend weeks at a time on a particular subject. At the end of each unit, the students are given a test to assess what they have learned and retained. Jesus responded, "For it is written." I appreciate the present tense. He could have said "it *was* written," but by using the present tense, He showed the Word's efficacy for dealing with our very present struggle with *sintimacy*. Remember, He is Immanuel, God with us.

Similarly, Jesus' very nature was being tried. Satan was trying to see what Jesus was made of, to see if He would remain faithful to God. Notice in the Scriptures that Jesus had not proclaimed his divinity. A voice from heaven declared the message. Satan, in essence, acknowledged that he knew who Jesus was by saying, "If you really are the Son of God..." Jesus was on trial defending His honor, and through His commitment to purity and dependence on the Word of God, the charges were dismissed and satan had to flee His presence.

Let's look at this again. The chart on the next page reveals the nature, source, and reasons for temptations, trials, and tests.

	Source	**Purpose**	**Related Scriptures**
Temptations	Internal to the believer	An enticement to move from the pathway of perfect obedience to the will of God	Matthew 26:40-42; Job 31; 1 Corinthians 13:10; Proverbs 14:12-16; 22:3-5; 1 Peter 1:4; 2:11; 2 Peter 2:10; Romans 1:24; 6:13; 7:5; Galatians 5:24; 6:8; Ephesians 2:3; 4:22
Tests	God or satan	To prove what you know or have learned	Deuteronomy 6:13-19; 8:1-5; 10:20; Joshua 24:14; 1 Samuel 7:3
Trials	God or satan	To prove your faith, innocence, guilt, or worth	Luke 8:12-14; 2 Peter 2:9-10; Genesis 39:7-10; Job 31; Psalm 1:4-6

The temptations are often revealed in the midst of our trials. Remember, in our trials, our internal mettle and worth are established. Our guilt or innocence is proven by our ability to withstand the temptations that come our way.

Let's look at temptation in its most common connotation: a secret, internal urging to commit some wrongful deed. In verses 14 and 15 of the first chapter of James, the writer described temptation as a sort of gestation and birthing process. As in the laws of attraction, where we are drawn to another human being through physical forces, temptation begins with a simple glance. Our minds can be pretty active; this is why we must guard ourselves against what we see and hear. Media images can last for years. That initial seed, if not aborted, develops, multiplies, and grows until it induces action (labor). When we learn to respond to tempting thoughts by stopping them at the door of our minds, evaluating them on the basis of God's Word, and dismissing those that fail the test, we have found the way of escape that the Scriptures promise.

In his letter to the Corinthians (10:6-10), the apostle Paul described five different types of temptations the Christian would have to endure: lust after evil things; being drawn towards idolatry, which includes self-centeredness; sexual immorality; the temptation to get Christ to serve us instead of serving Him; and the temptation to complain, again related to selfishness. These five also reflect the three overarching lusts.

Temptation does not occur simply because we have a desire, for we have many desires that go as fast as they came. Rather, temptation happens when those desires are not just fleeting ideas but capture us and cause us to say, "Yes, that would be good." And, by good, I do not mean a right thing but one we perceive to be appealing—even as Eve perceived the fruit to be both good and pleasing (Genesis 3:6). This is where the rationalization begins, for one is not thinking so much about what really is good but simply what seems positive at any given moment.

- **Illustrated with addictions:** A person who has been trying to quit smoking, or who has already kicked the habit, has a tough day at work and is super stressed. As he processes the day, he thinks about how soothing a nice, long drag would be. "Yeah, it would be good to have a smoke." Notice he has not decided to smoke; he has only decided to agree with his desire that this would be a good thing.

- **Illustrated with peer pressure:** A teenager goes to school. She sees all the cool people sitting together at lunch, laughing. She is alone. Inside is growing a desire to be accepted by that group. The thought does not leave but haunts her with every step. Every time she sees people, all she can think about is how "good" those kids have it and how nice it would be if she were one of the popular crowd.

These temptations can be very strong desires, and sometimes you may feel powerless over them—read Paul's struggle in the Book of Romans, chapter 7. The Lord has provided some protections in the Bible for overcoming or avoiding temptations. The Apostle Paul wrote about the importance of thinking about positive, godly thoughts in Phillipians 4:8-9. In 2 Peter 2:9, the scriptures read that "*the Lord knows how to rescue the godly from trials*" and 1 Corinthians 10:13 promises that "*with temptation [He will] provide a way to escape.*" Dealing, however, with this type of internal pressure without the power of the Holy Spirit and obedience to the word of God, the *sintimate* Christian cannot overcome sin and temptation. Maintaining God's righteous standards must become core matters in our daily walk. To that end, apply these principles when you come to the place of testing and temptation:

- Realize that through the word you have the power and authority to resist satan (John 15:3, 7);
- Memorize the word of God deep into your mind and spirit (James

1:21);
- Meditate (ruminate) day and night on the verses you have memorized (Psalm 1:2);
- At the very moment of temptation, speak the memorized word with authority;
- Obey the Spirit's prompting which will typically include removing yourself from the situation (Romans 8:12-14); and,
- Strengthen yourself through prayer (Ephesians 6:18).

B. Secret Sin and Its Impact

"What's the problem with secret sin? It's not hurting anyone but me."

"Oh, what a tangled web we weave when first we practise to deceive." (Sir Walter Scott, 1808; *Marmion, Canto vi. Stanza 17*)[3]

The above statements are two of the most prolific in understanding *sintimacy*. One is the excuse given to justify doing the wrong thing, and the other is the result of that justification. People who are battling *sintimacy* have a flawed values system. Their standards of desirability, goodness, rightness and truth are skewed. A person's values—their character, strength, and integrity—are most easily summed up by the following question: Who am I when no one is looking? Imagine what people would think about you if they knew all the things you do in secret. What would they call you? What would they say?

Secret sin is problematic for multiple reasons. One, it reveals major character flaws. The *sintimate* are liars, deceivers, untrustworthy, duplicitous, and, in a word, selfish. It is this self-centered, egotistic, it's-all-about-me attitude that flies in the face of God, who is supposed to be central to the Christian. God's focus is outward, selfless, caring for the needs and fulfillment of others. His children and ambassadors are supposed to reflect these same attributes. The church as a whole must war against the spirit of selfishness that has crept into the body of Christ. *Sintimacy* is a symptom of this sickness.

Additionally, secret sin is about dishonesty. Let's look briefly at the *Merriam-Webster Dictionary*[4] definitions for the word "secret:"

1. Kept from knowledge or view. Hidden sinful habits are marked by discretion, and the *sintimate* work with hidden aims or methods.
2. Remote from human frequentation or notice. Truthfully—as if truth exists in *sintimacy*—*sintimate* lifestyles are very lonely, as the perpetrator falls deeper and deeper.
3. Revealed only to the initiated. This is an interesting one. There are times when the *sintimate* will reveal his problem to another person. Often this person is either also caught up in the same problem or telling this particular person is inconsequential to the *sintimate*. Perhaps, the confidante is willing to cover up the other's sin.
4. Designed to elude observation or detection. Self explanatory. Who are you hiding from?
5. Containing information whose unauthorized disclosure could endanger security. For a moment, think about whose worlds would be shattered if they knew the depraved actions of your *sintimacy*.

In his letter to the Romans, the apostle Paul reveals the major problems with hidden lifestyles. In chapter two, Paul wrote:

> *"You who call yourselves Jews are relying on God's law, and you boast about your special relationship with him. You know what he wants; you know what is right because you have been taught his law. You are convinced that you are a guide for the blind and a light for people who are lost in darkness. You think you can instruct the ignorant and teach children the ways of God. For you are certain that God's law gives you complete knowledge and truth. Well then, if you teach others, why don't you teach*

> *yourself? You tell others not to steal, but do you steal? You say it is wrong to commit adultery, but do you commit adultery? You condemn idolatry, but do you use items stolen from pagan temples? You are so proud of knowing the law, but you dishonor God by breaking it. No wonder the Scriptures say, "The Gentiles blaspheme the name of God because of you"* (vv. 17-24 NLT).

Because of you, *sintimate* one, there are scores of people who deny the existence of God, who revel in their presumption of the number of hypocrites in the church. Because of you, the area of kingdom authority that you are supposed to have dominion over, your sphere of influence, grows increasingly smaller. Because of you, someone has refused the opportunity to get to know a loving, living Savior. I hope this fact bothers you. The selfishness of *sintimacy* clouds this very important fact: We live this Christian life to impact others. The apostle Paul wrote, *"The only letter of recommendation we need is you yourselves. Your lives are a letter written in our hearts; everyone can read it..."* (2 Corinthians 3:2). So, if you are the only Bible some will ever read, what facts of the saving power of Jesus Christ will they learn from your life?

The synonyms[5] for secrecy also are screaming examples of the attributes of a *sintimate* lifestyle:

- **covert** stresses the fact of not being open or declared
- **stealthy** suggests taking pains to avoid being seen or heard, especially in some misdoing
- **clandestine** implies secrecy, usually for an evil, illicit, or unauthorized purpose and often emphasizes the fear of being discovered
- **surreptitious** applies to action or behavior done secretly, often with skillful avoidance of detection and in violation of custom, law, or authority

- **underhanded** stresses fraud or deception

The *sintimate* need to understand this very important fact: Nothing is secret! Close to 100 scriptures in the Bible speak to God's harsh outlook on secret sin and lifestyles. We will review three such scriptures as examples.

Jesus Looks at Secrecy as Hypocrisy

"The time is coming when everything that is covered up will be revealed, and all that is secret will be made known to all. Whatever you have said in the dark will be heard in the light, and what you have whispered behind closed doors will be shouted from the housetops for all to hear!" (Luke 12:2-3 NLT).

God's Condemnation of Secret Sin

"He will judge everyone according to what they have done. He will give eternal life to those who keep on doing good, seeking after the glory and honor and immortality that God offers. But he will pour out his anger and wrath on those who live for themselves, who refuse to obey the truth and instead live lives of wickedness. There will be trouble and calamity for everyone who keeps on doing what is evil—for the Jew first and also for the Gentile...And this is the message I proclaim—that the day is coming when God, through Christ Jesus, will judge everyone's secret life" (Romans 2:6-9, 16).

What Happens in Secret affects You Publicly

"When you give to someone in need, don't do as the hypocrites do—blowing trumpets in the synagogues and streets to call attention to their acts of charity! I tell you the truth; they have received all the reward they will ever get. But when you give to someone in need, don't let your left hand know what your right hand is doing. Give your gifts in private, and your Father, who sees everything, will reward you. "When you pray, don't be like the hypocrites who love to pray publicly on street corners and in the synagogues where everyone can see them. I tell you the truth, that is all

the reward they will ever get. But when you pray, go away by yourself, shut the door behind you, and pray to your Father in private. Then your Father, who sees everything, will reward you" (Matthew 6:2-6).

As you can see, there is not much praise for secret behaviors in scripture. There is, however, encouragement to find a secret place to be alone with God. Overwhelmingly, Christians are called to live transparently so we become a prism to reflect the wonder of Christ's glory.

In the summer of 2008, former senator and presidential candidate John Edwards admitted his own *sintimate* behavior, an act of adultery. In his written statement, Edwards described one of the root causes and attributes of *sintimacy.*

> "It is inadequate to say to the people who believed in me that I am sorry, as it is inadequate to say to the people who love me that I am sorry. In the course of several campaigns, *I started to believe that I was special and became increasingly egocentric and narcissistic.* If you want to beat me up, feel free"[6] [italics mine].

We are only as sick as our secrets. When you are sick, the first thing you lose is your appetite. If you have no appetite for the things of God, check your spiritual health. During His earthly ministry, Jesus promised to give us abundant life here, in the natural. I believe He was referring to spiritual healthiness. Secret sin is contagious in the sense that what we do as individuals has significant impact on others. If there is something wrong with our relationship with God, then our effectiveness as a witness for Jesus is severely limited. If we are conduits for God's movement in the land, and our sin creates a barrier between us and God, then there is also a blockage between our sphere of influence and the presence of God. This should concern every *sintimate* Christian, as it thwarts the very plan of God to save the lost and dying.

We must get off the cycle of sin and begin to walk. When we are sitting in the chair like Goldilocks and it breaks, it will undoubtedly bring pain. Why do we wait until something hurts us (i.e.: our boss or our spouse finds us doing something wrong)? Why does it have to be that something has to get broken before we stop sinning (i.e., our relationship)? Why do we have to hit rock bottom before we see the need to stop doing that which is against the will of God? Eyes naturally gravitate towards the light. If Christians, who are called to be salt and light to this world, are living in the darkness of sin, then the lost who are naturally searching for us cannot find us. We must reflect the grace and mercy God desires to introduce to the world. This dramatically exemplifies the importance of having no separation between us and God.

◇◇

"The secret we want most to conceal is the one we need most to reveal."

◇◇

The secret we want most to conceal is the one we need most to reveal. The revelation we need is one where we break loose from the bonds of slavery to sin. As mentioned earlier, *sintimacy* creates in us a selfishness that produces spiritually hidden agendas. The Lord is prepared to offer amnesty, but He requires transparency and disclosure. In the last part of verse two of Psalm 32, David says God does all this for the one in "whose spirit is no deceit." That doesn't mean someone who has no faults, but rather refers to those who readily admit their sins. It's the idea of authenticity. It means we are not deceitful in acknowledging our sin. The key to Christian life is not our personal holiness, but our repentance. It's not a matter of trying to be perfect, but recognizing that we're not. We need to fully admit we are twisted transgressors and selfish sinners. Far too many of us are dishonest about our sins.

King David acknowledges the pain of secret sin in verse three of chapter 32. His physical body reacts, *"When I kept silent, my bones wasted away through my groaning all day long."* As he reflects on how he has failed to be open about his shortcomings, David felt like his bones were decaying. When we live in secret, our bodies react; we pretend to be normal and happy, while we are actually experiencing pain and misery. When we keep our mouth shut, our conscience screams. Proverbs 28:13 says, *"He who conceals his sins does not prosper."*

When you make a mess, confess. When you recognize your sin and reject it, God will remove it. In Psalm 32:5, David wrote, *"Then, I acknowledged my sin to you and did not cover up my iniquity. I said, 'I will confess my transgressions to the LORD'—and you forgave the guilt of my sin."* When David was ready to be totally free of his life of *sintimacy*, he made the important first step of confession. By bringing his dirty deeds to light, he was making the personal declaration and commitment to no longer conceal the sins he had been hiding. We can't expect God to cover what we're not willing to uncover.

If you're not ready to confess, then maybe you need more distress in your life. Call sin what it is. The solution is forgiveness. Until we acknowledge that what we've done is sinful, we won't experience freedom and restoration. The only way to be rid of our regrets and to have our sins covered is to confess them to God. Some of you have asked for forgiveness, but you're still pulling a suitcase of sin with you. Make the decision today to break the cycle.

In the Book of 2 Kings chapter 18, Elijah summoned the Israelites from all over to meet him at Mt. Carmel. When they had gathered, he asked them, *"How long halt ye between two opinions?"* The word halt has multiple meanings—lame, limping, stopped, paralyzed—none of which are very good. This double-mindedness (James 1:8) causes spiritual, personal, emotional, and mental instability, a disorder in which people become "unresolved under their convictions, unstable and unsteady in their purposes, promise fair, but do not perform, begin well, but do not hold on, that are inconsistent with themselves, or indifferent and lukewarm in that which is good." In short, *"Their heart is divided"* (Hosea 10:2); whereas, God will have all or none. The *sintimate* must acknowledge, and be rid of, the misery of this spiritual paralysis. Noted theologian John Wesley once wrote, "It is dangerous to halt between the service of God and the service of sin, the dominion of Christ and the dominion of our lusts. If Jesus be the only Saviour [sic], let us cleave to Him alone for everything; if the Bible be the Word of God, let us reverence and receive the whole of it, and submit our understanding to the Divine teaching it contains."[7]

In many ways, secret sin is the result of the lack of a pure heart that is connected to Jesus through prayer. When Elijah confronted the prophets of Baal, he called the Israelites near and *"repaired the altar of the Lord that was broken down."* The trouble in many churches is not the pastor or the program. The trouble is "broken altars" in the lives of God's people. Ahab and the people expected Elijah would, in this solemn assembly, bless the land and pray for rain—given that there had been a famine in the land for three-and-a-half years—but he had other work to do first. The people had to be brought to repentance and reformation, and then they could look for the removal of the judgment, but not until then. This is the right method. God will first prepare our hearts and then cause His ear to hear. He will first turn us to Him and then turn to us (Psalm 10:17; 80:3). You must not look for God's favor until your allegiance to Him is certain.

Before reading further, familiarize yourself with this story in 2 Kings 18, in which Elijah set his mind and hands to rebuilding the altar of the Lord. The *sintimate* must follow this example. Let us follow the pattern he used:

- Put God back on the throne of your life (Proverbs 3:1-6).
- Gather the people. Tell them your decision to live for Christ.
- Get one mind; no longer halt between two opinions (Deuteronomy 6:4-5).
- Repent (Revelation 2:4-5).
- Shun evil and unrighteousness (1 Thessalonians 5:22).
- Put the bull (sin and excuses) on the altar.
- Let the fire burn out the dross (impurities).

This process reveals an acknowledgment of the sovereignty of God as the One to whom we yield; a commitment to serving Him only; a public pronouncement of our allegiance; taking dominion and authority over sinful behaviors; and self control through the power of the Holy Spirit. Each of these concepts will be discussed in more detail later.

C. Sexual Sin

Imagine a young man who claims to be a devout Christian is caught up in a sexual relationship before marriage. One night, following their nightly tryst, the young lady expresses her love for the young man and her desire to be his girlfriend. The couple is still naked in the bed, and the young man states, "I cannot be with you because you are not saved" and tells her the plan of salvation. Imagine! You may be stunned, and possibly laughing at the incredulity of this event, but this true story is reflective of the blindness, foolishness, and delusion of *sintimacy*. It is also revelatory of the power of sexual sin and its controlling influence. Sadly, that young man was me.

I don't know about anybody else, but part of the reason I finally said "no more" (for good) was the fact that I finally recognized my *sintimacy* (pornography) was absolutely, beyond the shadow of any doubt, controlling me. Time to get personal. I first started experimenting with porn when I was seven or eight years old. (Sad, isn't it?) I can remember peering through the mail slot of a machine shop along my paper route. Inside, pictures of naked ladies were pasted to the walls and I could barely make out the images, but I could get a glimpse. If you are over 30 years old, you may remember how the premium channels on television were scrambled when mature adult content was playing. If you were like me, you would strain to see between the distorted images. I knew it was wrong, and I wish I would have realized how those stolen glances would plant seeds that would hinder my spiritual growth for years to come. The addiction to pornographic images in magazines, film, and on the Internet became a raging inferno within me. Years later, I would find myself a clandestine frequenter of adult bookstores. Regrettably, I know them all too well.

One such memory haunts me. I can remember vividly the time I was driving down the highway and one of those stores was a short distance away. I boldly proclaimed to myself, "No! I am not going to stop today." A few feet away—I was not going to stop. I started to pass the store as my mind was screaming "no-no-no," but an incredible compulsion overcame me, and I recklessly turned into the parking lot. I know what you're saying: "You didn't have to get out of the car." And you're right. However, I was being controlled. I'm not blaming the devil; I'm blaming my own sinful lust and desire. I have never moved so fast; in a lightning quick moment, my seatbelt was off and I was in the building.

That was the beginning of the end for me. It was scary being so out of control of my own desires, mind, and body. Notice I said "the beginning." I was still not dissatisfied. Why dissatisfaction? This is what indulging in secret sexual sin is all about: satisfying the lust of the flesh. What is satisfaction? It is the phenomenon of being full and contented. It has the same root as saturated. Stick a dry sponge in water and what happens? It will absorb all the liquid it can until there is no more room for anything else. This analogy is important.

Rev. James R. Bond, pastor of Revival Tabernacle in West Milton, Pennsylvania, challenges the common notion that "all sin is sin," comparatively speaking (e.g.: a lie is the same as stealing). His challenge is that sexual sin is a "sin of the body" and, as such, is more severe. I have had to think about this and have reasoned out the following:

We have all been created as sexual beings; it is a part of our physical and spiritual genetics. Have you ever noticed how strong the sex drive is? That's God's creation. We are predisposed to sexual desire. Our sex drives last well into our senior years, barring any medical condition. Yes, the drive is different for an octogenarian than a twenty-something, but a drive nonetheless. The problem with sexual sin is that it controverts the spiritually natural force with unnatural lust and desire, and what it produces is not life but death.

Additionally, the body is typified at the "temple of the Holy Ghost" (1 Corinthians 6:19), and as such, must be wholly pure and clean. When sexual sin sullies the temple, it creates a breeding ground for a resistant mold that is difficult to get rid of; you have probably heard of the term "soul ties" where through the physical, spiritual, and mental oneness of the sexual act, the partners are permanently connected. As a jealous God, the Savior does not need or want a roommate in his abode.

In 1 Corinthians 6:15-20, Paul describes the nature of sexual sin and how it breeds spiritual death.

> *"Know ye not that your bodies are the members of Christ? Shall I then take the members of Christ, and make them the members of a harlot? God forbid. What? Know ye not that he which is joined to a harlot is one body? For two, saith he, shall be one flesh. But he that is joined unto the Lord is one spirit. Flee fornication. Every sin that a man doeth is without the body; but he that committeth fornication sinneth against his own body. What? Know ye not that your body is the temple of the Holy Ghost which is in you, which ye have of God, and ye are not your own?*

> *For ye are bought with a price: therefore glorify God in your body, and in your spirit, which are God's."*

Through Christ's salvation, the human and the divine become intertwined. In fact, scriptures indicate that we become one with Christ and share of "*his body, of his flesh, and of his bones*" (Ephesians 5:30). We become joined together and our physical bodies become "*one Spirit*" with him (1 Corinthians 6:17). We are the "*temple of the Holy Spirit*" and, as such, the habitation of God, ostensibly the house of the Lord (1 Corinthians 6:19). Imagine someone bringing a pig into the temple during Old Testament times. That's just not kosher. Arguably, this would be a horrific gesture against the sanctity of the temple. Just as this action constitutes defilement of the physical temple, fornication—adultery, sodomy, and any sexual activity outside of the bonds of marriage—defiles the spiritual house of God. You may as well walk up to the throne of the Almighty God and spit in His face. Or consider it this way—Peter described how Jesus bore the sins of the world so we could live righteously (1 Peter 2:24). To be *sintimate*, then, is like sauntering up the Via Dolorosa to the bleeding, crucified body of the Savior and rubbing jalapenos into the wounds. Hollywood even speaks to the eternal significance of sexual sins of the body. In the film *Vanilla Sky*, one character mentions, "Don't you know that when you sleep with someone, your body makes a promise whether you do or not?"

It is for this reason I would argue that secret sexual sin is the single greatest killer within the body of Christ. Some argue that it is simply an offense between Christian brothers and sisters. An offense can be readily appeased; sexual connections are forever. Sexual sin has been described as "every man's battle." It is destroying Christians of all types, levels, denominations, and positions. Research indicates that 29-39 percent of Christian men have some sort of sexual addiction. We must also acknowledge how, like in my own personal experience, our super-sexual culture is overwhelming the younger generation and is interrupting God's plan to build His kingdom in our youth.

Recently, there was a veritable drought in our area; it had not rained for two or three months. (Picture grass that is parched, sun bleached and crunchy.) Walking on the grass with no shoes was painful. I was amazed that, amidst all the crackling dryness, the weeds were still growing. The grass had long died, and the weeds towered over it. This reminds me of how pervasive and strong the pull of sexual sin. Even when there is seemingly no life to be found, the desire continues to grow. How does it happen with no rain or nutrients in the ground to draw on? I'm no botanist, but I have a feeling the weeds continue to grow *because* they suck the life out of the grass around them until all that's left is dry and good-for-nothing-except-the-burn-pile. And it hurts.

What is the difference between a yard and a lawn? My neighbors have lawns; one religiously manicures his land each Sunday morning. His wife plants only the choicest of greenery and flowers; her garden grows the most scrumptious-looking vegetables. The couple to the right hires landscapers who regularly weed, mow, prune, shape, design, and trim. There is typically not a blade or leaf out of place. Both plots of land are reminiscent of photographs seen in *Better Homes and Gardens;* each reflecting the care and pride of the residents. My yard, on the other hand, is the unkempt epitome. I must be an embarrassment to these masters of lawn maintenance. My spot of land gets cut maybe twice a month; each ten steps lead to a different patch of some overgrown thicket. The neighboring lawns are green and healthy; my yard is blotchy at best. Fallen limbs abound on my property, the kids' toys lie abandoned, and there is no shortage of weeds.

While cutting my yard the other day, I found myself surrounded by a cloud of wishing flowers. You remember these, right? When we were kids, we would pick them, make wishes and blow the seeds into the wind. We used to play a game with these dandelions gone to seed. We even had a song.

"Momma had a baby, and its head popped off." Dandelions typically don't survive in a lawn, but flourish in a yard. What people often forget is that dandelions are weeds and you need to get rid of them before they spread. How do they spread? Left unattended, they change their look and become pretty little wishing flowers, and the unsuspecting—perhaps children or a soft wind—come by and pretty soon, you have many more dandelions.

Our spiritual lives should be treated like the lawns of my neighbors; we must tend to it so that the right flowering fruits grow. We must regularly remove weeds (and learn to tell the difference between weeds and true flowers). We must be diligent about the upkeep so that our neighbors can see the beautiful image of the homeowner.

D. Walking in Darkness

1 John 1:5-10 reads as follows:

> *"This is the message we heard from Jesus and now declare to you: God is light, and there is no darkness in him at all. So we are lying if we say we have fellowship with God but go on living in spiritual darkness; we are not practicing the truth. But if we are living in the light, as God is in the light, then we have fellowship with each other, and the blood of Jesus, his Son, cleanses us from all sin. If we claim we have no sin, we are only fooling ourselves and not living in the truth. But if we confess our sins to him, he is faithful and just to forgive us our sins and to cleanse us from all wickedness. If we claim we have not sinned, we are calling God a liar and showing that his word has no place in our hearts"* (NLT).

To walk in darkness means to live in sin and immoral pleasures. Such people do not have fellowship with Him (i.e.: they are not born of God). Those who have fellowship with Him experience God's grace and live a life of holiness in the presence of God. Intimacy with Christ produces a continual cleansing.

It is important to note how John uses the noun *sin* rather than the verb (i.e.: "we do not sin") to emphasize sin as a principle in human nature. John is probably arguing against those who affirm that sin does not exist as a principle or power in human nature or those who say the evil actions they commit are not sin. Believers must be aware that the flesh, or our sinful nature, is a constant threat to our lives and we must always be putting to death its evil deeds through the Holy Spirit who dwells within (Romans 8:13; Galatians 5:16-25).

Christians have lost the concept of living for perfection and being consumed by godliness. We seem to have a preference for halfway rightness—which also means halfway wrongness. I preached a message once entitled "Walking in Limited Light." It was an evening service, and as I rose to the podium, I asked the ushers to turn off all the lights in the sanctuary. Once it was dark, I asked the congregation to turn in their Bibles to the scriptural text for the day and read it aloud. Naturally, there were cries of "We can't see" and "It's impossible to read this in the dark." I probably could have concluded the sermon right there. It is impossible to do the things of God, such as read the Bible, while walking in darkness. Yet, thousands of us try. Later, I turned on a lamp I had on the platform so I could see my notes. The congregation stayed in the dark, although my light helped them a little. When the ushers turned the lights back on at the conclusion of my message, there were anguished cries of pain as people's eyes tried to readjust to the light. This is our exact response when God turns His light on our sinful lives; we want to retreat to the darkness where we were more comfortable (Romans 13:11-14; Proverbs 16:2-3; 1 Corinthians 4:5; Ephesians 5:8).

When we're talking about being in the darkness or walking in the wilderness, we're talking about living in sin and serving our immoral pleasures, our evil desires. What is frightening is that we serve sin with delight. Oftentimes, when we get into *sintimacy*—in the going from "too hard" to "too soft" to "just right"—we begin to see we derive a sense of pleasure in trying to find the thing that fits us just right. You know you're living a *sintimate* life when you lose the sense of conviction; it no longer bothers you to do what you're doing. The loss of sensitivity to the spirit of conviction has seriously impacted both personal and corporate kingdom growth. Furthermore, it is one of the building blocks to deeper levels of spiritual development. By way of example, let's look at Ezekiel 47:1-12:

> *"Then the man brought me back to the entrance of the Temple. There I saw a stream flowing eastward from beneath the Temple threshold. This stream then passed to the right of the altar on its south side. The man brought me outside the wall through the north gateway and led me around to the eastern entrance. There I could see the stream flowing out through the south side of the east gateway. Measuring as he went, he led me along the stream for 1,750 feet[a] and told me to go across. At that point the water was up to my ankles. He measured off another 1,750 feet and told me to go across again. This time the water was up to my knees. After another 1,750 feet, it was up to my waist. Then he measured another 1,750 feet, and the river was too deep to cross without swimming. He told me to keep in mind what I had seen; then he led me back along the riverbank. Suddenly, to my surprise, many trees were now growing on both sides of the river! Then he said to me, "This river flows east through the desert into the Jordan Valley, where it enters the Dead Sea. The waters of this stream will heal the salty waters of the Dead Sea and make them fresh and pure. Everything that touches the water of this river will live. Fish will abound in the Dead*

> *Sea, for its waters will be healed. Wherever this water flows, everything will live. Fishermen will stand along the shores of the Dead Sea, fishing all the way from En-gedi to En-eglaim. The shores will be covered with nets drying in the sun. Fish of every kind will fill the Dead Sea, just as they fill the Mediterranean! But the marshes and swamps will not be purified; they will be sources of salt. All kinds of fruit trees will grow along both sides of the river. The leaves of these trees will never turn brown and fall, and there will always be fruit on their branches. There will be a new crop every month, without fail! For they are watered by the river flowing from the Temple. The fruit will be for food and the leaves for healing."*

Wherever you are in your relationship with God, I am here to tell you, it's not enough. I believe God would rather have us in a deeper, even more committed relationship with Him. The scriptures we just read indicate there are more levels to which God would take us. It is important to note that the law, and expectations, of God go beyond conviction and repentance.

In this passage, Ezekiel is being led by the angel of the Lord, and these verses reveal the levels of being in the Spirit. The angel has a measuring line and denotes four depths of the water: to the ankles, the knees, the loins, and overhead. The first level, where the waters are at the ankles, can be termed the level of conviction. At a very basic level, we recognize we're getting wet. We're standing in the water. (Biblically, water is used to connote the Spirit.) At this spiritual level, we feel conviction that we're doing something wrong. Ankle-deep water can be likened to the baby pool. And what do we remember about being in this pool? Playing and splashing around. Spiritually, being in ankle-deep water is a relationship with God that it about conviction. When we're convicted, it means we're in a place of guilt and judgment. When we're at this level, it is easy to come to church—when we feel like it. We may come to hear the singing or when there's an altar call. We only get close enough to splash around. We're satisfied to get a touch from the Lord. At this stage, it's all about fun, not about changing. When here, a person expects the Lord to bless him or her but doesn't expect to give up anything in return. The angel says this is not enough and directs us to a deeper level.

He measures out an additional line to where the water comes to the knees. It is important to note that the water is at the knees because typically, this is the place of humility in prayer. We kneel before God in the submissive act of repentance. A part of the process of repentance is acknowledging we're in a sinful state and standing before a holy God. In a sinful state, we're unable to continue in the presence of the Lord (Psalm 24), so we have to humble ourselves to be exalted through repentance. This stage is still pretty shallow. The water is just to the knees, which leaves plenty of room to splash and play. Now, don't get me wrong. Repenting from our sins is important, but we must be willing to go beyond repentance. In fact, the Scriptures teach us this in Hebrews 6:1-2:

> *"Therefore leaving the principles of the doctrine of Christ, let us go on unto perfection; not laying again the foundation of repentance from dead works, and of faith toward God, Of the doctrine of baptisms, and of laying on of hands, and of resurrection of the dead, and of eternal judgment."*

The angel of the Lord leads us to a deeper place than repentance. The man measures out another 1,000 cubits (1,750 feet), and the waters come to the level of our loins. Now we're starting to get somewhere. We're getting ready to go into the deep end of the pool. We're crossing the line demarcating the swimmers from the novices. At this stage, the water is about waist high. The spiritual description for this stage is conversion.

In the book of Acts, Peter gives the following instructions: *"Repent and be converted that your sins may be blotted out"* (3:19). What does it mean to be converted? The loins region is the area where our nature resides. It is the place from which life flows. Think biologically. Women birth children from the loins; men plant seeds of life from the loins. Our natures can be described as our primitive state, our fundamental disposition or temperament. Our human nature and predisposition is such that it is typically opposite from God's. Paul mentioned that our flesh often wars with the spirit, a constant struggle of good versus evil. To convert means to change, and this is what God wants. The water at the loins means we're being converted and changed from what we used to be. When we are born again, Scriptures teach us that we "put on Christ" (Romans 13:14) and are made anew (2 Corinthians 5:17). Further, when Christ returns, we'll be changed again. We'll shed this mortal and put on immortality. Corruptible will put on incorruptible. (1 Corinthians 15:52). At this stage, we're getting there. It is a good thing to submit to the will of God and allow God to change us, but still, that's not enough.

Having our nature changed is a constant struggle, so the Spirit leads us to a deeper place where we're no longer in control. The waters are deep enough to swim in. In the deepest waters, the current is so strong that even the strongest swimmers have difficulty going against it. Spiritually, this is the place of sanctification. Now we're swimming. God would have our relationships with Him at this level. At this stage, we're no longer reliant on our own powers and abilities. In Romans 12, Paul refers to this process as being "transformed by the renewing of your mind" (v. 2). This mind renewal occurs so we can be assured of knowing that which is good, acceptable, perfect, and in the will of the Lord for our lives. Secret sin is none of these things.

Now, it's in this place where our minds are renewed, where we're no longer in control and we're led by the Spirit, that we're stronger than our weaknesses. The apostle Paul stated, "In my flesh, there is no good thing." So, alone, we cannot control ourselves. Willpower alone is insufficient, although we must make the choice to live for holiness; our will must be subject to God's will. Solomon stated we are not to "lean on our own understanding" (Proverbs 3:5) because we're faulty. This notion of sanctification requires us to yield to God's authority and direction. In water rescue training, lifeguards are taught to teach the struggling or drowning person to surrender to the current and allow it to carry them; fighting against the current only makes you tired.

Also of note is that, in the deeper waters, the heart is covered. The heart is the seat of our wills and emotions. It is also the place where all blood flows, and blood is the sustainer of life. If the heart stops, life ceases to be. This reflects a necessity of having a heart change. Interestingly enough, several times in the Greek translations of the Scriptures, the word mind is the same as the word heart. So, having a renewed and transformed mind may also refer to having a pure heart. In Psalm 51, David prayed, *"Create in me a clean heart, O God, and renew a right spirit within me."* This is why it's easy for people to go back into sin; their heart has not been renewed, and the right spirit is not present. If the heart is impure, then everything that ensues from it is also impure.

A vital aspect of God's purpose for us involves our coming to repentance, recognizing our sinful state and how far short we fall of God's standards, and determining to begin living God's way of life. We strive to identify and overcome our sins and live a sin-free life. In 1 John 3:9, the apostle John tells us, *"Whoever has been born of God does not sin, for His seed remains in him; and he cannot sin, because he has been born of God."* We should understand several points from this verse. In his plan for overcoming sin, John Meakin argues, "First, the converted Christian does not habitually sin. He has, after all, turned away from sin. The sense here is not that a Christian will never sin; we remain human, imperfect and subject to the pulls of our nature and a degenerate world around us. Instead, the sense is that a Christian will not remain in the practice of sin."[8]

However, when God helps us recognize the enormity of our sins, a natural human response is dejection and discouragement. Even the apostle Paul struggled with his weaknesses, lamenting that *"in me (that is, in my flesh) nothing good dwells; for to will is present with me, but how to perform what is good I do not find...The evil I will not to do, that I practice"* (Romans 7:18-19).

Many fail in their fight against sin by attempting to overcome it by their own strength rather than relying on God's Spirit. Paul acknowledges this human deficiency. He knew full well the impact of the law of human nature and conduct. *"Evil is present with me, the one who wills to do good,"* he wrote in Romans 7:21. This scripture describes the struggle of Paul's—and every Christian's—corrupt nature with his new godly nature.

A second point of this scripture is that God's Spirit is like sperm—it is the source of spiritual life. When we are pregnant with the spirit, we possess the power to not commit sinful acts. When God's seed remains in us, we are enabled to live righteously. This does not mean that we will not occasionally fall off the horse, but that with God's help, we can overcome sin's dominion.

Sanctification is often described as being "set apart for God's purposes," and this is an accurate depiction. However, another definition of the word sanctify is "to make productive of holiness or spiritual blessing."[9] This is an important definition because, in the remainder of the verses, it speaks to the production of life that is brought about by the river's flow.

> *"Suddenly, to my surprise, many trees were now growing on both sides of the river! Then he said to me, "This river flows east through the desert into the Jordan Valley, where it enters the Dead Sea. The waters of this stream will heal*

> *the salty waters of the Dead Sea and make them fresh and pure. Everything that touches the water of this river will live. Fish will abound in the Dead Sea, for its waters will be healed. Wherever this water flows, everything will live..."*

In his vision, Ezekiel sees a life-giving river coming out from the temple. As it flows, it grows in depth and width, giving life and fruitfulness to everything it touches. The river flows into the Dead Sea area and rids it of its death. The purpose of the river is to bring abundant life and healing from God to the land and the people. This river is similar to the river flowing from the Garden of Eden and the River of Life in the New Jerusalem that flows from the throne of God.

This river is also similar to the one mentioned by Jesus. *"Whoever believes in me as the scriptures has said, streams of living water will flow from with him"* (John 7:38). The living water is the Holy Spirit and the blessings of life He has come to bring. Read these words from of Hebrews 5:

> *"Concerning this we have much to say which is hard to explain, since you have become dull in your [spiritual] hearing and sluggish [even] slothful in achieving spiritual insight]. For even though by this time you ought to be teaching others, you actually need someone to teach you over again the very first principles of God's Word. You have come to need milk, not solid food. For everyone who continues to feed on milk is obviously inexperienced and unskilled in the doctrine of righteousness (of conformity to the divine will in purpose, thought, and action), for he is a mere infant [not able to talk yet]! But solid food is for full-grown men, for those whose senses and mental faculties are trained by practice to discriminate and distinguish between what is morally good and noble and*

> *what is evil and contrary either to divine or human law"* (vv.11-14 AMP).

The writer of Hebrews is speaking specifically to the *sintimate* Christian. Our relationship with Christ should be so deep that secret sin is not a factor. God wants us to move on to maturity. How far are you willing to go to remove *sintimacy* from your life?

What I advocate is a revolution, a revolt against sin. At the heart of all revolutions in history is a movement to overthrow oppressive tyranny. This is where we must start. As I see it, revolution does not just happen. Do you know what the number one step to revolution is? Go ahead; take a moment to think about it. My answer is dissatisfaction. We will never get to the revolutionary stage until we get dissatisfied with our oppression and the oppressor. Had the original settlers not been dissatisfied with their way of life in England, they never would have sought the New World. Once here, had the British government not saddled them with high taxes and levees, there would not have been a war fought for independence. Let's face it: People involved in secret sin are not yet dissatisfied. Oh, I know, you feel guilty and horrible *after* you have fallen. How come no one ever feels guilty beforehand—enough not to sin—or during the act? It's only after we have pleasured ourselves that we have moments of regret. When will we truly be sick and tired of being less than holy?

We get bothered by our *sintimate* failures after the fact, even though God sent the way of escape, the moment of conviction, long before the moment of temptation. We choose to ignore the warnings: the billboards, the nudge, the blaring horns, whatever it might be. The things we want to do take precedence over the warning signs. In truth, the *sintimate* want to serve the *sintimacy* with delight; we just like doing what we do. Otherwise, we wouldn't do it. What we need to understand is what Paul stated: Such people do not have fellowship with God.

In his second letter to the Corinthians, the apostle Paul wrote, *"If any man be in Christ, he is a new creature. Old things have passed away and behold all things are become new."* To be in Christ means to be so wrapped up in Him that we cease to be our own. It means to be so completely enthralled that: 1) we acknowledge Him in all our ways (Proverbs 3:6) and 2) we are led by the Spirit of God. To be in Christ means to be purchased, for Christ to be involved in our lives.

We're talking about living in sin. We have already mentioned that one act of sin led to the downfall of all mankind. We have to get it into our heads that one act of disobedience is one too many for those who want to be in Christ. Because we live in the dispensation of grace, we like to think, "Oh, I'll be alright because God loves me, so I'm just gonna go ahead and do what I want to do." While grace is a reality, this type of thinking is faulty because God lets us know He is jealous, has high expectations, and it is a terrible thing to make Him angry. I am thankful His grace is such that He tempers His wrath with His mercy.

We quote the scripture "*For the wages of sin is death, but the gift of God is eternal life through Jesus Christ our Lord*" (Romans 6:23). It is important for us to recognize that we think we're getting away with our *sintimacy* because we don't get shot down, or our limbs don't fall off, or our eyeballs don't fall out (Old Testament-style judgment). Please understand that, although you don't hear the audible voice of God telling you to stop whatever you're doing, it still means death for you. This is important to remember because, if you have lost the spirit of conviction, that urging against the *sintimate* actions, your death is imminent.

He that is led by the Spirit of God will not fulfill the lust of the flesh. If you are not being led by the Spirit, you are not going to hear the spirit of conviction. You need, however, to go beyond conviction, because, in my estimation, conviction only makes us feel bad. Typically, we feel bad, but we do the thing anyway—and then we feel worse. We cry, "Oh, I hate myself. I should just give up. I can't win. I can't beat this thing. I'm never gonna stop." When we get to this place, we stay stuck. So conviction, in and of itself, is not enough. We also need to understand the importance of repentance.

Please begin to pray in earnest for that spirit of conviction to return.

> *Lord, when I am getting near the place—long before I get there—please alert me with the siren, the bullhorn, whatever You need to do to let me know that where I am heading is not right.*

E. Powerlessness, Helplessness, and Guilt

I invite you, my reader, into my secret thoughts of almost 15 years ago as I wrote an essay to the Lord regarding my *sintimate* ways. I had just graduated from college and was in the first month of graduate school. I was also working with a youth program on campus for the summer. You will no doubt feel my frustration and sadness. In fact, reading it now, I wonder if I was considering suicide. In this letter, I express my regret to God for having failed time and time again. I wanted to recognize His call on my life, but my *sintimacy* was overwhelming me. I can still see myself that evening in my dorm room typing this on my word processor. The title I gave the essay was "*Master, Can You Use ME?*"

> This week, I have had to do some serious soul-searching. I have never been so introspective and deep "in the valley" in my life—well, in a long time. You see, I am at that stage in my life where nothing seems to be going my way, nor do I see any purpose or direction for my existence. I just recently graduated from college—with honors, awards, recognition, etc., but my life seems to be going nowhere, except maybe downhill. No job prospects, a graduate school that I didn't/don't want to attend, and most of all, a nearly estranged relationship with God.

The only thing that has brought me or brings me any joy was my relationship with my girlfriend, but right at this point in my life, even she cannot bring me solace. You see, she lives in Long Island, NY while I live in Western PA.

I have been in the church all my life—raised in the Baptist church until my father died (I was 5), then my family joined the "grand ole" Church of God in Christ. I got saved in the Baptist church (baptized too) on May 4, 1980—so I know about the ways of the church. It wasn't until August of the same year that I first heard of the baptism of the Holy Ghost. I remember receiving that very special gift under the tutelage of an anointed woman of God, Mother Mamie Williams. Boy, did I tarry (pray really hard) that morning!

Unfortunately, that was over fourteen years ago my first experience with the Lord. Oh, how I long for the zeal and passion for godly things that I had then. The problem that I face (or, one of the problems) is that I, like so many "saints"—especially in the Holiness, Pentecostal, and Charismatic movements is stalemate(ness) [sic]. I have been in the church "way" for so long, and as a good friend of mine said once, we know how to "act saved." Like Paul taught against in Philippians 4, we who have been saved for so long think we have "attained." And I've come to know that when you have attained is exactly when the devil uses you the most. Why? Because when you have attained, you stop reading your Word, prayer time diminishes, and your total relationship with God dwindles. Church services aren't the same because your passion is gone and you feel like you've heard all the messages that have ever been preached; they all just seem to say the same thing. So, as I stated earlier, "devilment" is the easiest recourse. It gives you something to do, especially when you are supposed to be in your prayer closet.

This is why may heart has been so heavy laden this week. In all of this craziness that I have not-so affectionately termed "MY LIFE," the things of God are mainly peripheral. I think I am one of those musical Christians. (A musical Christian is one whose spiritual relationship is based on music. When you hear a really moving gospel jam, then you begin to feel the Spirit). Nevertheless, I feel totally useless—naturally and spiritually.

How can God use someone like me? I have been on the religious roller coaster for so long, and I am starting to get nauseated. The sometimes-up, some (most)-times down cycle is wearing me down. I wonder if I'm truly of any earthly good, or as Paul said, "O, wretched man that I am." It's like no matter what I do, it always ends up being wrong. I really don't intentionally mean to sin, nor do I set out to do wrong, but "every time I try to do the right thing" evil is ever present and I succumb (sometimes I fight the good fight, other times it's a simple renege). So by the end of it all, the devil has won a victory and I'm stuck because the devil has now convinced me that I couldn't be saved or I'm just destined to be a hypocrite.

The bad thing is the face that I know the Lord has called me to a life of ministry. But how can I be a minister of the gospel when my anointing s based upon the spiritual yo-yo? Sometimes I try to justify my actions by saying "This will actually help me as a minister because I can now effectively and honestly teach against it because I've experienced it firsthand." But NO sin can be justifiable for any reason! So, how, with all this darkness hovering about and around (even, in) mecan I be used of God?

I truly want to be saved all the way. In the words of that old time church song, "Lord I'm striving, trying to make 100. 'cause 99 ½ won't do." I'm not happy in this state, and as a child of the Almighty, I deserve a minute amount of happiness and peace of mind. Anyway, I really want to be used, but as I said before, I feel worthless to everyone, and mostly to God.

Prayer: Lord, is it possible for you to use someone like me? I know that I'm no good and often displease you by the things I say and do, but I need you. I can't live without you. Amen.

Lately, I've been trying to come up with a solution to this problem. I know ultimately that I must strengthen my relationship with God, but I feel I've sunk so low that I need to start from scratch. I know the word says in Revelation 2:4-5:

> *"Nevertheless I have somewhat against thee because thou hast left thy first love. Remember therefore from whence thou art fallen, and repent and do the first works; or else I will come unto thee and will remove thy candlestick out of his place, except thou repent."*

But what does it mean by first works? Is he saying that I need to start over, or do I take up right where I left off? I've tried the latter and I have had some success. But here I am again. Now what?

I think my best solution would be to get back to grass roots. As a matter of fact, this might be a solution for anyone in my category—finding a new, renewed, improved love for the Word of God. That should be really easy for me because I'm a teacher (or so I believe my calling to be) and I love the things one can learn. But I find it hard to concentrate and focus on the Bible on a consistent basis like I ought. Anyway, my next step should be to get an honest, sincere prayer life. But you know what amazes me, after all these years, I still don't know HOW to pray. I mean pray like Rod Parsley or T.D. Jakes means pray. I've heard the term "seeking God's face" but few times have I ever achieved that goal effectively.

Then too, I think a total change of mind is necessary for me. As

I was reading Lord, Change Me by Evelyn Christenson, she wrote about how the Lord had to give her a change of mind such as one in Romans 12:2, "But be ye transformed by the renewing of your mind that ye may prove what is that good, and acceptable, and perfect will of God." That is the primary way of getting the anointing back. But, the biggest key for me right now is leaving the sin business alone, by getting out of those situations that will lead to trouble.

Prayer: Almighty and Gracious Father, please accept me, even in my wretched state. I repent of my wrongdoing. Please forgive my sins of omission and commission, of those things that I have sinfully hidden in my heart or that I have done in the privacy of locked doors. I need your forgiveness. I'm nothing without you. Please give me back the passion I shared for you and the anointing of your presence in my life. Restore unto me all those things which I've allowed the devil to steal from me. I submit my life to you. Let thy will be done. Amen.

"Create in me a clean heart and renew a right spirit within me."

As I mentioned earlier, my path towards destruction started very early in my life; I struggled for at least two decades with the constant, nagging pull towards anything pornographic. I could not help myself. The letter you just read was written while I was working at an academic summer camp. I was particularly frustrated with myself because of yet another moral failure. I could not help myself. Failure after failure after failure—I could not help myself.

You probably sensed my desperation. I heard the Spirit telling me to give it up and let it go. Nothing seemed to work. I knew there was a calling on my life; I was born to deliver God's Word. How could I be the man God expected yet still be drowning in secret sin? Could God still use me? Why didn't God just strike me down with His giant lightning bolts? I wished for an Old Testament reprisal; *then* I would stop. Once I lost an eye or came down with a mysterious case of leprosy, I would "just say no" and declare my victory. I am so thankful God did not respond like that.

Anyone who has been wrestling with secret sins knows how powerless we sometimes feel when faced with our greatest temptations. I know what it is like to feel powerless. One of the most significant feelings is that of inadequacy, feeling totally ineffectual. The powerless have a range of emotions: hopelessness, emotional exhaustion, detachment and withdrawal, isolation, irritability, frustration, being trapped, failure, despair, cynicism, and apathy.

If you're powerless and the helplessness expresses itself as irritability, you might find yourself snapping at people or making snide remarks about them. If the burnout manifests as depression, you might want to sleep all the time or feel too tired to socialize. You might turn to escapist behaviors such as sex, drinking, drugs, partying or shopping binges to try to escape your negative feelings. Your relationships at work and in your personal life may begin to fall apart. You may lose your trust in others, believing people act out of selfishness and nothing can be done about it. In a nutshell, for the *sintimate*, powerlessness manifests itself in the following ways:

- Blunted emotions
- Helplessness and hopelessness
- Loss of motivation, ideals, and hope
- Detachment and depression
- Emotional distress
- Despondency and feeling like life is not worth living

Regrettably, the powerless often make excuses for their behaviors. They often feel there is no chance for deliverance, so it becomes very easy to just give in. In the late 1800s, Robert Christy stated, "He declares himself guilty who justifies himself before accusation."[10] Gabriel Meurier, in

1970, wrote, “He who excuses himself, accuses himself.”[11] Shakespeare expressed it as “…oftentimes excusing of a fault/Doth make the fault the worse by the excuse”—King John, act IV, scene ii, lines 30–31. Each of these great thinkers revealed the heart of powerlessness: excuses. We negate the power of God when we succumb to temptations and continually live in sin. What amazes me is the number of Christians who try to justify their wrongdoing by giving scriptural justification. They say, *“For all have sinned and come short of the glory of God”* (Romans 3:23) or *“There is not a righteous man on earth who does what is right and never sins”* (Ecclesiastes 7:20). Imagine, throwing God’s Word up in His face like that! Most people who choose to revel in the fact that *all have sinned* readily ignore the preceding and following verses in Romans 3 which speak to our ability to live righteously according to God’s standards.

The apostle Paul, the writer of most of the New Testament, described his own struggles with the problems that would not go away. Paul wrote the following:

> *“But I need something more! For if I know the law but still can’t keep it, and if the power of sin within me keeps sabotaging my best intentions, I obviously need help! I realize that I don’t have what it takes. I can will it, but I can’t do it. I decide to do good, but I don’t really do it; I decide not to do bad, but then I do it anyway. My decisions, such as they are, don’t result in actions. Something has gone wrong deep within me and gets the better of me every time. It happens so regularly that it’s predictable. The moment I decide to do good, sin is there to trip me up. I truly delight in God’s commands, but it’s pretty obvious that not all of me joins in that delight. Parts of me covertly rebel, and just when I least expect it, they take charge. I’ve tried everything and nothing helps. I’m*

> *at the end of my rope. Is there no one who can do anything for me? Isn't that the real question?"* (Romans 7:17-24 *The Message*).

Paul's frustrations with his own struggles mirrored my own. Paul basically said there was a war going on in his mind and body. He wanted to do right and good, but somehow he kept on messing up. Paul mentioned that, no matter what he tried, the sin always seemed to be there. Don't feel defeated by this, though. The apostle Paul did not quit because he had some shortcomings and messed up on occasion. He could have given up, but he chose to rely on God's Spirit to help him. In fact, when Paul thought of this ongoing battle within, he asked, *"What shall we say then? Shall we continue in sin...?"* (Romans 6:1). He answered his own question and said, "God forbid"—or "No way!" (6:2) and that, because of the Spirit of God living inside us, "we should not serve sin" (6:6). The Spirit came to make us "free from the law of sin and death" (8:2). Furthermore, God will give us the power and desire to continue to obey Him (Philippians 2:13). Get in the habit of continually fighting to do what's right, even if it is a struggle.

God will help us by His Spirit to win the battle. Zechariah 4:6 reminds us that the secret to winning the battle is "*'not by might, nor by power, but by my spirit,' says the Lord.*" Paul negates his own powerlessness by reminding himself that Christ's suffering and ultimate resurrection enables us to live holy lives above our own besetting sin. In Romans 7: 25, Paul wrote, *"The answer, thank God, is that Jesus Christ can and does. He acted to set things right in this life of contradictions where I want to serve God with all my heart and mind, but am pulled by the influence of sin to do something totally different."*

Chapter Three
Breaking Free

No More Secrets

In November 2006, the Christian and secular worlds were shocked to hear about the illicit behaviors of Ted Haggard. After his *sintimacy* was revealed (sexual impropriety with a male prostitute and alleged drug abuse), Haggard became public enemy number one. In the offing, a number of lives were impacted. What can we learn from his mistakes?

It is not my goal to pass judgment on my brother for, therefore, I am intentionally not adding much commentary or explication, other than highlighting revelatory statements. In public statements released by the overseers of his church, Haggard's wife Gayle, and Haggard himself, we have an additional case study to examine the causes, definitions, and results of a secret, sinful lifestyle. I want you to draw some of your own conclusions, particularly in the light of your own *sintimate* behaviors.

Ted Haggard[12]
"I have further confused the situation with some of the things I've said during interviews with reporters..."

"I am guilty of sexual immorality, and I take responsibility for the entire problem."

I am a deceiver and a liar. There is a part of my life that is so repulsive and dark that I've been warring against it all of my adult life.

"*...from time to time, the dirt that I thought was gone would resurface*, *and I would find myself thinking thoughts and experiencing desires that were contrary to everything I believe and teach.*"

"*Then, because of pride, I began deceiving those I love the most because I didn't want to hurt or disappoint them."*

"The public person I was wasn't a lie; it was just incomplete. When I stopped communicating about my problems, the darkness increased and finally dominated me."

"I created this entire situation. The things that I did opened the door for additional allegations. But I am responsible; I alone need to be disciplined and corrected."

"I am a sinner. I have fallen. I desperately need to be forgiven and healed."

"*Because of the negative publicity I've created with my foolishness, we can now demonstrate to the world how our sick and wounded can be healed..."*

"*We will never return to a leadership role at New Life Church."*

Overseers at New Life Church[13]
"*...we have decided that the most positive and productive direction for*

our church is his [Haggard's] dismissal and removal. In addition, the Overseers will continue to explore the depth of Pastor Haggard's offense so that a plan of healing and restoration can begin.

Gayle Haggard[14] (in a letter addressed to the women of New Life)
"I know your hearts are broken; mine is as well."

"For those of you who have been concerned that my marriage was so perfect I could not possibly relate to the women who are facing great difficulties, know that this will never again be the case."

Questions to consider:

- In what ways are we defined by our actions?
- How do we break the curse of our past secret sins?
- What may be the challenges of coming clean (telling others) about secret sins?
- Regarding Haggard, his private sins have been made public information. What would you say are the consequences for him, personally, professionally as a minister, and to the body of Christ?
- Proverbs 24:16 reads, *"For a just man falleth seven times, and riseth up again: but the wicked shall fall into mischief."* How can someone who has fallen so many times be declared just?
- 2 Corinthians 5:17 declares, *"If any man be in Christ, he is a new creature: old things are passed away; behold all things are become new."* What does it mean to be in Christ, and, if someone continues to struggle with a particular sin or problem, does this mean he is not in Christ? Justify your answer.
- What advice would you give a person so crippled with the guilt of sin that she feels she can't break free from her problem? (Can you back up your answer with scripture?)

What Haggard's letter reveals is what has been coined by Rev. Rob Brendle of New Life Church in Colorado Springs (Haggard's former church) as the "whack-a-mole method" of sin management. Far too many *sintimate* people are simply reactive to their acts of *sintimacy*, feeling guilty and sorry after the fact. They then cry and pray and make promises to God. Rather than looking deep inside for the root cause of *why* we are drawn to certain elements or activities, sin managers just wait until the bad acts pop up. Don't you find it interesting that, when something goes awry in one part of our lives, doing the thing we don't want to do becomes so easy? A person who is trying to give up smoking is most likely to smoke after a stressful day. I can hear them say, "Oh, if I could just have a cigarette that would make this stress go away." These things are connected, and we must understand that no pervasive, secret sin stands alone. It is largely interconnected with some other root. Sin management is not the method to be preferred; we must stay vigilant and on guard. When we are prepared, we are less likely to falter.

It is important, then, to be willing to examine what is happening in other areas of our lives rather than looking only at the episodic symptoms. This is akin to taking aspirin for recurring chronic headaches. The root cause may be a brain tumor, but we continue to treat the manifesting problem. We must be cognizant of the motives and patterns that accompany our behaviors. What was going on in the days or moments leading up to the stumble or fall? Being aware of and deconstructing the preceding feelings and thoughts as the antecedent reactions can give clues into the prevention and cure. This is the appropriate place to state that a good Christian counselor can be very helpful in uncovering roots and deep-seated issues.

Accountability

One of the most difficult choices a person who is getting free from *sintimate* activities must make is deciding to out oneself. The self-help and recovery programs all identify "acknowledging that you have a problem" as a primary step in the recovery process. This acknowledgment takes on a very different tone when you are talking about telling someone else about secret sin. This public announcement by alcoholics and those addicted to drugs or other substances is not news to most of the people around you. Our families and friends know when we are struggling with these trials. Imagine telling your significant other, your children, and your congregation that you are struggling with some secret sin, especially something sexual in nature. Frightening thought, huh? I will go on record as saying that going public, to those whom you trust initially, is absolutely essential for continued freedom. I've already mentioned the dangers of secrecy, but it bears repeating that the enemy would love you to remain silent about your *sintimacy*.

How do you decide to tell and to whom do your reveal this secret? It's as tough to decide as it is to do. There are multiple ways to reveal and multiple reasons to or not to. You should know that there is great potential for people to be hurt, confused, and angry at you. They may also feel betrayed.

I'll be honest with you; revealing *sintimacy* is scary. What's more are the looks of surprise and dejection that can appear on the faces of those with whom you share this news. I know what you're saying right now: "I don't want to hurt so-and-so. Therefore, I won't tell them." Trust me, friend, this is a trick of the enemy. Besides, if you didn't want to hurt that person, you shouldn't have put yourself in this position in the first place. Before you cop out, hear this: That person deserves to know; some of our hidden faults put them in danger, too. Read here John Edwards' 2008 statement about coming clean to his family:

> "In 2006, I made a serious error in judgment and conducted myself in a way that was disloyal to my family and to my core beliefs. I recognized my mistake and I told my wife that I had a liaison with another woman, and I asked for her forgiveness. Although I was honest in every painful detail with my family, I did not tell the public.

> When a supermarket tabloid told a version of the story, I used the fact that the story contained many falsities to deny it. *But being 99 percent honest is no longer enough.*"[15]

Telling my own wife about the depth of my addiction and the levels of depravity was one of the most difficult things I had to do. I had to stare into those eyes that were my normal place of comfort and praise, only to reveal what I knew would cause tears to come. Sitting in our kitchen, not only did I have to confess my depravity, but in the interest of full disclosure, I had to tell her the numerous ways I had lied to her to do what I wanted to do. I will never forget her face. I saw not sadness, but a terribly angry pity. I expected her to yell and rant at what a coward I had been, at how I was a failure. Imagine my surprise when she shared feelings of inadequacy as a wife. She reported how my failures meant she must not have been a good wife and had failed me in some way. Imagine! I was the one with the moral failures; I was the one who was committing sin and betraying her trust, but she was blaming herself. Friend, your actions do impact others. Your secrecy directly harms those you say you love.

I also had to tell my oldest son. He didn't know I knew about his struggles in the same arena. I couldn't scold him—or so I thought—for doing the same thing I was doing. So, rather than being a conscientious parent, I let him wallow in the muck, too. I couldn't hold out anymore. Both our freedoms were in the mix. I told him that I knew about his problem and that he needed to stop using the family computer for viewing pornography, not only because it was wrong and that his younger siblings had access to the same computer, but because I, too, was trying to stay clean and could not afford to take the chance of seeing his files. His expression was one of shock. James 5:16 reads, "*Confess your faults one to another, and pray for one another, that ye may be healed.*" I never did find anymore of his files on the computer. I certainly hope my disclosure helped. Again, Paul writes, "*To the weak I became as weak that I might gain the weak*" (1

Corinthians 9:22). This is a sign that we need to share the scars of secret sin with others, first, for accountability and second, to save someone else from the same pain.

I mentioned earlier about the nature of *sintimacy*, only revealing our problems to those who are initiated. I found it easy to confess to guys whom I knew struggled in the same area. That's what we do when we are not really serious about changing. You see, those guys would be able to empathize with my failures. They would pat me on the back and commence to share with me how they, too, had struggled or failed that week. Yes, in some convoluted way, I was being accountable to these men. I let them in on my dirty little secret. If I was honest with myself at that time, I probably would never have told them if I didn't already know they struggled, too.

This type of fake accountability system doesn't help. Just because someone knows about your problem, does not guarantee freedom. Oh, we would get together and pray about the struggle, but none of us would call each other at the moment of temptation—only after failing. The goal of accountability systems is protection from failure, not a pity party afterwards. Additionally, your accountability partner(s) should be given access to your life and thoughts. They should know your temptations and weaknesses. You need to eliminate secrets. The best accountability systems are those where your partner can ask you any real question about your issue and you would be completely frank and open.

It is important to note that your accountability partner should not be your best friend. This is not the person with whom you go golfing or shopping or out for coffee on a regular basis. This person must be able to see the real you, beyond the holiness smoke and mirrors you try to put up. This is not the "Hey, how are you doing? Nice weather we're having" type of conversation. The person holding you accountable should challenge you spiritually. There are conflicting opinions about whether this person needs to have been delivered from a similar problem as yours. This may be helpful, but that deliverance should not have come in the recent past. This person needs to live that freedom on a regular basis. Regardless, your accountability partner should have the following attributes:

- Committed to prayer (for self and others)
- Full of the Holy Spirit and showing fruit of a spiritual life
- Honest and willing to speak the truth
- Discreet (not the neighborhood gossip)

Additionally, I would add that, because of the sensitive nature of most accountability relationships, opposite sex partnerships are frowned upon; no sense adding fuel to a glowing fire. And for people who are really serious about changing, we recommend choosing someone you are embarrassed to tell (i.e.: your mom, pastor or wife). If you are serious about changing, then pick a serious accountability partner.

Some great questions your partner should regularly ask include the following:

- What problem has consumed you this past week?
- Which direction is your personal relationship with Christ going?
- How have you been tempted this past week?
- Do you feel emotionally drawn or vulnerable to someone other than your spouse?
- How have your times in the Word and prayer been?
- Have you been diligent in areas of agreed-upon personal discipline?
- Have you lied to me in any of your answers?

You should also spend time in prayer and Bible study. The concluding chapter of this book offers scriptures that speak to a variety of *sintimate* behaviors.

Understanding Your Temptation Triggers

"If you think you are standing strong, be careful, for you, too, may fall into the same sin" (1 Corinthians 10:12).

Part of your continued freedom will depend upon knowing and understanding your triggers. These are your vulnerability points. A trigger is anything that makes you vulnerable to your former lusts or behaviors: perhaps sudden stress, pain or discomfort, or a glimpse at a magazine. (I sometimes have to avoid looking at women's clothing and undergarment catalogs.) This may also include the acknowledgement that some of your personal relationships may need to change. Sometimes, even hanging around with certain people makes us vulnerable.

We need to understand that once a trigger event happens, we can have some level of internal dysfunction. These symptoms can include difficulty thinking clearly, managing feelings and emotions, and moments of remembrance when we mistakenly see our former behaviors as positive. The recovery specialists refer to this as euphoric recall: We remember the "good" but ignore the immensity of the negative.

On His last night of earthly ministry, Jesus and His disciples had retired to the Garden of Gethsemane to pray. Before breaking off from the group for a few moments of solitude, Jesus spoke to His disciples and said, *"Watch and pray, that ye enter not into temptation"* (Matthew 26:41). Here Jesus taught us that being aware of the possibility of temptation is the effective method of staying out of trouble. He knew it is easier "never to" than break the habit. Put it this way: Goldilocks would never have gotten into danger if she had not entered the wilderness in the first place.

I want to point out again that temptation itself is not sin. In essence, a temptation is just a thought that pops into our heads—most often as a result of carnal living. It is when we consider that thought as a viable option that it becomes sin. So, the battle starts in the mind. Do you have your battle gear on? The last vestments of the whole armor of God as defined in Ephesians 6 are *"the helmet of salvation and the sword of the Spirit, which is the Word of God"* (v. 17). I find it interesting that salvation is what guards the mind. When tempting thoughts arise, start fighting with this declaration: I'm saved! This statement reflects the resurrecting power of Jesus Christ. In that declarative statement, we acknowledge that, according to Romans 6:2, we are dead to sin. When we learn to stop tempting thoughts right at the outset, we will find greater success in the battle.

As you know, there is typically a pattern to our thoughts triggered by temptations. So, let's interrupt our thought processes towards evil deeds and develop a new strategy for victory. Philippians 4:8 defines a proactive and reactive approach to the thoughts that enter our minds. Paul writes that we ought to fill our minds and meditate on *"whatsoever things are true, whatsoever things are honest, whatsoever things are just, whatsoever things are pure, whatsoever things are lovely, whatsoever things are of good report."* Regularly thinking about these things can be preemptive as they rid our thoughts of wickedness. They also provide an excellent manner of judging the worth or appropriateness of any particular activity. Go ahead; pause right here and think about your temptations. Do they pass muster in light of this passage? When you are tempted, quickly scrutinize whether the thought, if it became action, would be pure, right, truthful, honest, etc. Would you be able to give a good report (think about standing in front of your congregation and testifying) if you did the action? Does it line up with God's Word, His will for your life, and your purpose as a witness for Christ?

Once we become skilled at testing the merit of a tempting thought, we must be willing to "take the hard right instead of the easy left" and not give in to the desire. Making this decision shows our willingness to follow Christ. It also shows that we are actively engaged in our own emancipation. Read this advice from the wise King Solomon: *"A prudent person sees trouble coming and ducks; a simpleton walks in blindly and is clobbered"* (Proverbs 22:3 *The Message*). God promises the escape route, but we have to take the turn to avoid trouble.

When all else fails—run! Did you know the Bible gives us an out in the face of temptation? Check these out:

- Flee fornication (1 Corinthians 6:18).
- Flee from idolatry (1 Corinthians 10:14).
- Flee these things (1 Timothy 6:11).
- Flee also youthful lusts (2 Timothy 2:22).

Quit trying to act like Superman or Wonder Woman. You are not less of a man if you say you can't handle the situation. God would rather you be wholly holy than worry about some mythic notions of masculinity or femininity. Even superheroes have weaknesses.

In the face of temptations, consider the following assessment:

And whatsoever ye do in word or deed, do all in the name of the Lord Jesus, giving thanks to God and the Father by him (Colossians 3:17).

The Bible teaches that following the leading of the Spirit is crucial for righteousness, holiness, avoiding failure, and being one who overcomes. The following guidelines offer a method for living a principled walk with the Lord. And since the Bible does not speak out against 21st century-specific sins, this list of questions can help determine the right path to follow. In everything we say, do, think or enjoy, we must ask the following questions:

- Will it give God glory? Does it reflect His attitudes, behaviors, or power? (1 Corinthians 10:31).
- If Jesus was standing next to me, would I do it? Would I do the action "in the name of Jesus?" (John 14:13).
- Would I ask God's blessing upon the activity? Would I offer Him

thanks for it?

- Would Jesus himself have done the activity while living on earth? (1 John 2:6).
- If another Christian saw me doing this, how would I feel? How would that Christian respond to seeing me? (1 Corinthians 8:9-13).
- Will it weaken my desire for spiritual things, God's Word, and prayer? (Luke 8:14; Matthew 5:6)
- If an unsaved person saw me doing the act, how would I respond? How effectively would I be able to witness to that unsaved person? Could I introduce Christ to that person while doing the activity? (Matthew 5:13-16).

So much of arresting temptations before we become agents of sin is determined long before the moment of temptation. We must make up our minds that we are alive in Christ and dead to a life of sin. The following scripture references indicate a predetermined attitude to honor God with our whole mind, body, soul, and spirit:

Genesis 39:7-10

"And about this time, Potiphar's wife began to desire him and invited him to sleep with her. But Joseph refused. "Look," he told her, "my master trusts me with everything in his entire household. No one here has more authority than I do! He has held back nothing from me except you, because you are his wife. How could I ever do such a wicked thing? It would be a great sin against God." She kept putting pressure on him day after day, but he refused to sleep with her, and he kept out of her way as much as possible."

Nehemiah 4:9
"But we prayed to our God and guarded the city day and night to protect ourselves."

Job 31:1
"I made a covenant with my eyes not to look with lust upon a young woman."

Job 31:19-34
"Whenever I saw someone who was homeless and without clothes, did they not praise me for providing wool clothing to keep them warm? If my arm has abused an orphan because I thought I could get away with it, then let my shoulder be wrenched out of place! Let my arm be torn from its socket! That would be better than facing the judgment sent by God. For if the majesty of God opposes me, what hope is there? Have I put my trust in money or felt secure because of my gold? Does my happiness depend on my wealth and all that I own? Have I looked at the sun shining in the skies, or the moon walking down its silver pathway, and been secretly enticed in my heart to worship them? If so, I should be punished by the judges, for it would mean I had denied the God of heaven. Have I ever rejoiced when my enemies came to ruin or become excited when harm came their way? No, I have never cursed anyone or asked for revenge. My servants have never let others go hungry. I have never turned away a stranger but have opened my doors to everyone. Have I tried to hide my sins as people normally do, hiding my guilt in a closet? Have I feared the crowd and its contempt, so that I refused to acknowledge my sin and would not go outside?"

Daniel 1:8

"But Daniel purposed in his heart that he would not defile himself with the portion of the king's meat, nor with the wine which he drank: therefore he requested of the prince of the eunuchs that he might not defile himself."

Say what you will about the efficacy of the 12-step programs, but one of the concepts they teach can be very effective in avoiding, escaping, and overcoming temptation: unconditional abstinence no matter what. When we are freed from the bondage of sin, we need to steer clear of anything that looks or smells like the former temptation. What happens so often, unfortunately, is that we intentionally go looking for the "close enough line." For instance, after a season of success, a person who was freed from a pornography addiction will not go to the XXX section of the video store, but will get a racy R-rated movie that is simply "soft porn" rather than hardcore. The person gets the same thrill with less guilt—and a little bit of self-righteousness—because, after all, he didn't get the porn. We must not go looking for reasons, ways, and excuses to relapse into old behaviors. Complacency and self-confidence are the enemies. Don't get too comfortable and forget the enemy does not want to see you free.

And that brings up the craving factor. The Bible mentions the existence of familiar spirits. In some ways, the nature of recurrent temptations and cravings is reflective of these familiar habits trying to creep back into our lives. You should know that the enemy will tempt us with what is familiar, not with what is strange or foreign. That's why the book of Hebrews talks about the sin that easily besets us. The deprivation causes cravings to intensify. I've heard former smokers speak of how just watching someone take a drag makes them desire to light up. Similarly, someone delivered from a food addiction—or even someone on a strict diet—might see a favored food and have a mini-meltdown. After a period of time, the cravings lose intensity and the easier it is to stand up to them.

"I can do all things through Christ who gives me strength!" (Philippians 4:13).

Taking Authority and Dominion

I am a big fan of movies, and one of my favorites is *The Wiz*. You have probably seen *The Wizard of Oz*, the movie that made Judy Garland a household name. *The Wiz* has quite a star-studded lineup, including Diana Ross as Dorothy; Nipsy Russell as the Tin Man; Richard Pryor as the Wiz; Lena Horne as Glinda, the Good Witch; and Michael Jackson as the Scarecrow. As one writer puts it, *The Wiz* is "an adaption of *The Wizard of Oz* that tries to capture the essence of the African American experience."

The stories don't vary much from each other: Dorothy is transported into a magical land; kills a witch; the witch's sister gets mad and tries to kill Dorothy; Dorothy meets some friends who are each looking for some external validation; they dance and sing their way to the Emerald City to speak to the great and powerful Wizard of Oz.

Soon after arriving in Oz, Dorothy learns she has accidentally killed the Wicked Witch of the East, and is rewarded the ruby slippers worn by the decedent. Dorothy is instructed to never remove the slippers until she returns to her native country (in this case, Harlem, New York). Evillene, the Wicked Witch of the West, goes to great lengths to coerce Dorothy into giving her the ruby slippers, which apparently hold great power. She tortures Dorothy's companions and even threatens to throw little Toto into a fiery furnace. Seeing her friends in peril, Dorothy is confused. Should she just ignore the instructions and save her friends? Just then, the Cowardly Lion yells out, "Don't give up the shoes, Dorothy!"

"Don't give up the shoes!" What a profound statement from such a cowardly creature. It reveals an important lesson for the *sintimate*: Our salvation is a treasure and should be guarded with every ounce of our beings. In essence, the Lion's admonishment was to hold onto the very thing that gives us overcoming power. You see, even Evillene with all her magic was powerless against those shoes. When she tried to use her powers to take the shoes, her fingers folded backwards and crippled her hand. Dorothy was untouchable as long as she was wearing those ruby slippers. Those shoes would become the symbol of Dorothy's authority.

Similarly, the body of Christ must learn to operate within the realm of kingdom authority that we have been given. In the Genesis account, when God created Adam, He gave Adam one thing: dominion (Genesis 1:28-30). When Adam sinned, his punishment was a loss of God's life within him: moral and spiritual death. Their former relationship to God was destroyed, and consequently, satan gained dominion, becoming the prince of this world (John 16:11). The grace of God is such that, when Christ died, He took dominion and gave it back to us (Romans 6:9, 12). We must recognize the battle of our souls is about one thing: dominion. Who is going to have control of your life and future? Through Christ, you have it. Satan wants it back, but don't give in.

Romans 6 teaches that Christians are dead to a sinful lifestyle. Amazingly, the *sintimate* prefer to resurrect that lifestyle. Our bondage and slavery to sin's dominion was broken by the cross of Christ, and we are called to walk in newness of life (6:4). Regarding dominion, Paul gave us these instructions in verses 6-14:

> *"Could it be any clearer? Our old way of life was nailed to the cross with Christ, a decisive end to that sin-miserable life—no longer at sin's every beck and call! What we believe is this: If we get included in Christ's sin-conquering death, we also get included in his life-saving resurrection. We know that when Jesus was raised from the dead it was a signal of the end of death-as-the-end. Never again will death have the last word. When Jesus*

died, he took sin down with him, but alive he brings God down to us. From now on, think of it this way: Sin speaks a dead language that means nothing to you; God speaks your mother tongue, and you hang on every word. You are dead to sin and alive to God. That's what Jesus did. That means you must not give sin a vote in the way you conduct your lives. Don't give it the time of day. Don't even run little errands that are connected with that old way of life. Throw yourselves wholeheartedly and full-time—remember, you've been raised from the dead!—into God's way of doing things. Sin can't tell you how to live. After all, you're not living under that old tyranny any longer. You're living in the freedom of God" (The Message).

These verses make an important declaration regarding our dominion in Christ. There has been an exchange: death to life, bondage to freedom, etc. Our continual freedom is dependent upon us making an exchange of behaviors. If we want to break the curse of *sintimacy*, we must change our behavior. In Ephesians 4, the apostle Paul shows us the manner of putting away the old life. In verses 17-29, Paul describes this new life. Having "learned Christ" (v. 20), Christians should "put off concerning the former conversations the old man" (v. 22). Conversations here refer to the manner of lifestyle, not just speech, although this should reflect Christ as well. He described a renewal of our thought patterns (Ephesians 4:23-24; Philippians 4:8) that would lead to changed behaviors.

Many people view the Bible as a series of "thou shall nots" instead of "thou shalls." Living this Christian life is not just a cancellation of activities we might enjoy. When I was a young professional, I used to do parent and family counseling. I would often teach parents not just to say no to their children, but also to offer them a yes. In other words, avoid just telling them not to do something; give them the correct alternative. Paul is doing the same thing for us in Ephesians 4. To those who are thieves, Paul instructs them to steal no more (v. 28). They are also instructed to pick up a new behavior that reflects the changed mindset. He says to let the former thief work for a living so that he may give to those in need. If you have a problem with lying, Paul teaches you to put away lying and begin to speak the truth. Got a potty mouth? Paul admonishes you to change your manner of speech to "that which is good to the use of edifying [others]" (v. 29).

I point this out in reference to Jesus' teaching in Matthew 12:43-45 and Luke 11:25-27 on the reality of evil spirits searching for a home. In these scriptures, Jesus speaks to the idea that, when a man is delivered from the possession or influence of a demonic being, the evil spirit roams about until it can find a new dwelling. If it cannot find a new home, the spirit returns to its former domicile and finds it fully cleaned and swept out (delivered), but nevertheless empty. According to these scriptures, the evil spirit goes to get seven even more evil friends to occupy the man with him. The man's condition is worse than it was before he was delivered. As believers, we must not just be satisfied with conversion, salvation and deliverance. Because the enemy is searching for a dwelling place, we cannot afford to be empty. If we are full of the indwelling Spirit of God and an unwavering commitment to Christ, dogged obedience to His Word, prayer, and righteous living, the enemy will find no vacancy to occupy and wreak havoc.

While I'm on the subject, Paul's instructions in Ephesians 4:25 to *"put away lying, speak every man truth to his neighbor"* is biblical proof that secret sins are against the plans of God for our lives. When we are living a double—or triple—life, we are not living truthfully before our neighbors.

In the middle of all these instructions, Paul makes a definitive statement that each of us seeking freedom must adopt: *"Neither give place to the devil"* (v. 27). You've heard the proverb "Give him an inch; he'll want to be a ruler."

The key, as the Lion told Dorothy, is not to give up what was given to us as the scepter of authority. Our symbol of authority? Self-control. Our ability to govern ourselves, to have mastery, is our God-given right and duty. Kings and other potentates have the ability to make whatever decision suits their fancy at a given time. In the same manner, we must make the decisions that are reflective of our authority and dominion. This includes choosing to do right, not being governed by carnal desires. I want you to note that the final fruit of the Spirit is temperance, which is self control. The Holy Spirit comes to give us the ability to be our royal selves. As royalty, we have access to all this in the kingdom, but we must remember *"All things are lawful unto me, but all things are not expedient: all things are lawful for me, but* I will not be brought under the power of any" (1 Corinthians 6:12). I just love the statement made by the writer of Acts, who stated, *"...and herein do I exercise myself"*—or, my rule as an authority—*"to have always a conscience void of offence toward God, and toward men"* (Acts 24:16). The Amplified Bible puts it this way, *"Therefore I always exercise and discipline myself [mortifying my body, deadening my carnal affections, bodily appetites, and worldly desires, endeavoring in all respects] to have a clear (unshaken, blameless) conscience, void of offense toward God and toward men."*

Blamelessness is a crucial element and weapon for spiritual success (2 Corinthians 1:12; 1 Timothy 1:19). There is a freedom revealed in having a clear conscience because we know God is not being offended by our thoughts and actions (Psalm 32:1; 1 Timothy 1:5; 1 Peter 3:16; 1 John 3:21-22). When I was living *sintimately*, I was always concerned—scared to death, actually—about being found out. My soul would shudder each time my wife said, "We need to talk." My mind would race to figure out what website she might have seen or what magazine or video she had found. Now that I am free, though, those words don't make me run for the hills. In fact, when she says, "We need to talk," I can stop and simply respond, "Yes, babe?" Liberation is amazing!

I want to return to this climactic scene in *The Wiz* for a moment. As I mentioned, Dorothy was considering giving up because it appeared all hope was lost. All of her friends were facing death and destruction, and she could not see a way out. The Lion's words stopped her on her path towards conceding. Moments later, as one of the witch's henchmen was carrying Toto towards the furnace, Dorothy pulled the fire alarm (in this film, the witch was running a sweatshop in a dilapidated warehouse), which turned the sprinklers on. The witch screamed and declared she was allergic to water and began to melt into her throne, which was actually a giant bronze toilet. After Evillene's demise, the water began to wash away the filth from the windows and the sunlight began to shine through. A breeze began to blow away the dust and dirt from the floor. Soon, the imprisoned, hideously deformed, sweatshop workers began to be transformed. Their prison was not one of cells and bars, but grotesque costumes that covered them from head to toe. As the water ran and the sun shone, what had once been dark and ugly, what had been binding them, began to fall off. The workers emerged from the cocoons of bondage and glistened in their new golden outfits that reflected the sunlight. When they realized their enemy was no longer a threat, they cheered and broke into song and dance. (*The Wiz* is a musical after all.) Their song of choice was entitled "Can't You Feel a Brand New Day?" The scene was reminiscent of a good, old-fashioned Pentecostal praise service.

I would like to offer a few pointers on retaining your authority based upon this example set by Dorothy and her pals:

- **Guard your treasure** (2 Corinthians 4:5-7).
  In Psalm 119:11, David declared, *"Thy word have I hidden in my heart that I might not sin against thee."* David valued the treasure of the Word and put it away for safekeeping.
- **Stand your ground** (2 Thessalonians 2:12-15; Romans 8:27-29; Hebrews 10:22).

The enemy will try everything to get you to give up your treasure. He will try to remind you of your past failures and lure you with temptations, but be strong and courageous. God is with you. Remember how Jesus responded to the devil's assault: "for it is written…" The treasure itself is powerful.

- **Know your enemy's tactics and his weaknesses** (Psalm 68:1; Luke 4:3-5; John 10:10; 1 Peter 5:7-8).
  Your enemy's job is to throw obstacles in your path. Avoid those things that steal, kill, and destroy the life of God inside you. The book of James suggests a surefire method: *"Submit yourselves therefore to God. Resist the devil, and he will flee from you"* (4:7).
- **Be washed in the Spirit; stay clean** (Isaiah 4:3-4; Galatians 5:1; 2 Peter 2:19-21).
  The book of Ephesians refers to being washed by the Word, and numerous scriptures reference being led by the Spirit of God to ensure you will not fulfill the lusts of the flesh. Your freedom is dependent upon following the commandments and directives of the Lord. His Word is a lamp and light.
- **Take off the old garments** (John 11:38-44; Isaiah 61:3).
  When Lazarus was raised from the dead, the first instruction Jesus gave was to remove his grave clothes. Lazarus would have looked mighty silly wandering around in his mummy outfit. He was no longer dead. Why should he look like he still belonged in the tomb? He whom the Son sets free is free indeed. Don't let the former death restrict and poison your present and future life.
- **Remember to praise God for freedom** (John 5:14; Luke 17:11-19).
  Honestly, when you emerge from the bondage of *sintimacy*, guilt and shame are very tangible—even months or years after, there are still so many regrets. Nevertheless, you should get in the habit of thanking God that you are not still bound. Every single time

I pass by an adult bookstore I used to haunt, I pause and thank God for delivering me. And, just so you know, I still get disgusted and remorseful as I pass by. I haven't forgotten the depth of my depravity. But even with those feelings, I am comforted and revel in the fact that those places no longer control me. My wife mentioned once that she got angry when I would praise God as we drove by the old spots. For her, they served as a painful reminder, too. That is my fault, and I accept it. She has forgiven me (I believe that with all my heart), but I cannot expect her to forget. I don't really want her to because she helps with my accountability even now.

Personal Responsibility

"God said to [Joseph] in the dream, "Yes, I know your intentions were pure, that's why I kept you from sinning against me; I was the one who kept you from going to bed with her" (Genesis 20:6 *The Message*).

One of the greatest difficulties of the *sintimate* life is overcoming our own excuses for doing the wrong that we do. We blame the devil, our peers, God, stress at work, kids or spouses who keep nagging us, anybody but ourselves. We blame Adam for eating the apple. We claim that it was unavoidable, that it was just an honest mistake. We say, "Hey, I'm only human." Oh, here's one: "The spirit is willing, but the flesh is weak." Couple these excuses with the feelings of hopelessness and powerlessness, and we get "Oh, I am just a bad person; I may as well do it anyway because I can't fight the feeling."

As long as we do not accept blame and responsibility for our wrongs—and for not doing right—our prayers of repentance are lacking. We must confess our sins—all of them. I watch *Law & Order* incessantly. Before District Attorney McCoy accepts a plea bargain, he generally requires the defendant give an allocution, formally and fully explaining the crime that was committed. The criminal cannot leave out any details, must include motives and thought processes, the who, what, when, where, why, and how of the criminal's actions. Without the details, McCoy has the right to reject or rescind the offered deal.

I am reminded of a story in John's Gospel of an infirmed man sitting by the pool at Bethesda waiting for a miracle. He had been crippled most of his life, at least until he had an encounter with Jesus. Read the story found in John 5:

> *"After this there was a feast of the Jews; and Jesus went up to Jerusalem. Now there is at Jerusalem by the sheep market a pool, which is called in the Hebrew tongue Bethesda, havingfiveporches. In these lay a great multitude of impotent folk, of blind, halt, withered, waiting for the moving of the water. For an angel went down at a certain season into the pool, and troubled the water :whosoever then first after the troubling of the water stepped in was made whole of whatsoever disease he had. And a certain man was there, which had an infirmity thirty and eight years. When Jesus saw him lie, and knew that he had been now a long time in that case, he saith unto him, Wilt thou be made whole? The impotent man answered him, Sir, I have no man, when the water is troubled, to put me into the pool: but while I am coming, another steppeth down before me. Jesus saith unto him, Rise, take up thy bed, and walk. And immediately the man was made whole, and took up his bed, and walked: and on the same day was the Sabbath. The Jews therefore said unto him that was cured, It is the Sabbath day: it is not lawful for thee to carry thy bed. He answered them, He that made me whole, the same*

> *said unto me, Take up thy bed, and walk. Then asked they him, What man is that which said unto thee, Take up thy bed, and walk? And he that was healed wist not who it was: for Jesus had conveyed himself away, a multitude being in that place. Afterward Jesus findeth him in the temple, and said unto him, Behold, thou art made whole: sin no more, lest a worse thing come unto thee."*

This is a very familiar story. We've heard it for many years. We're familiar with the location of this story: a pool called Bethesda. The pool was surrounded by five porches and on these porches, lay the sick and infirmed: the blind, the lame, those with diverse types of diseases. It is said that, at certain times, an angel would trouble the waters of the pool and the first person to enter the troubled water would be healed of their ailment. Enter Jesus.

Realizing the man had been by the pool for a very long time, 38 years, Jesus was moved to ask him a question: "Do you want to get well?" A simple question that, I would think, required a simple answer: yes or no. But the man had a very common human reaction: He gave excuses. The first excuse was that he had nobody to carry him to the pool. The second was that somebody always beats him to the punch. I am intrigued by these particular excuses, in that they are all too familiar in the present day church—especially for the *sintimate*. "It's somebody else's fault I'm in the condition I'm in."

For a moment, I want you to put yourself in this man's place—infirmed for almost four decades and all of a sudden, help shows up. Your helper asks, "Do you want to be healed?" How would you respond?

Although Jesus knew the man had been ill for a long time and also knew what was in his heart (John 2:24-25), He nevertheless initiated the contact by asking if he wanted to get well (5:6). In this story, we see an act of divine sovereignty, but what is also very clear is the importance of human responsibility, God's will meeting man's will. Jesus' question was another designed to reveal what was in the man's heart.

What would you say to Jesus if He asked you whether you wanted to be healed of your illnesses, physical or otherwise? Do we want to be rid of our addictions and other sins? Ten minutes hard thought on this question could lead us to new depths of repentance. It seems like a silly question; of course he would want to be healed. But, perhaps, the man had grown accustomed to his disability and preferred the known pain to the terror of the unknown with its new responsibilities.

God finds each of us as helpless as this man. The good news is He desires to grant each of us life, not necessarily mere healing in this life, but eternal life beginning now.

I want, for a moment, to go back to his excuses. The man said he was basically helpless. Everybody who surrounded the pool was in the same situation: sick and afflicted. No one cared enough that he was in bad shape; all were seeking the same healing. The man was there with no one to help him. So there was an unpredictable source of healing that could affect only a few people, and this man had no hope of getting healed because he couldn't get to the pool. In other words, this was a situation of utter hopelessness and futility.

It's important to note that, while the man could not get to the pool, Jesus could get to him. The man was met by the one who is the stable, constant source, not just of healing, but of life itself—eternal life. It is also important to note that Jesus typically healed as a response to the faith of individuals. This man did not even know he was talking to Jesus. He just thought it was a stranger who was well enough to carry him to the pool at the right moment. Here, however, Jesus required no faith at all. The man was cured merely at the word of Jesus. This illustrates the point that our human requirement is "reasonable" (Romans 12:1); little is needed on our part for God to work. Jesus' response was very simple: "Get up and walk." I imagine that, after 38 years of a debilitating disease, this man's bones and muscles had become weak. Yet, Jesus expected him to just get up. But when the man responded, he was completely healed. What a miracle! Those who knew this man understood the gravity of his illness, but taking up his bed (the site of his problem) and walking away from it proves his complete healing and deliverance. A simple response: "Get up!" Remember to run to do the will of God.

I think it is significant to mention the latter part of this story. Where did Jesus find this man later? In the temple. What a response! Healed from an affliction of almost four decades, I would imagine he would be running through the city doing all the things he couldn't do for so long. I imagine he would have had some wild oats to sow; but, no, his response was to be in God's house. How much we can learn from him!

Jesus saw him there and spoke (verses 14-18): "You got your deliverance. I freely gave it to you. Now, change your life. Stop sinning or else something worse will happen to you." Something worse than being an invalid for 38 years? Friends, hell is real, and Jesus is trying to tell us to avoid that place. Change your life now. He is saying to you, "I have already healed you of your affliction. Now let it go and don't do it anymore." If you are professing to be a child of God, a believer and follower of Jesus the Christ, then stop sinning. The truly regenerated will stop. Your path towards perfection may have some bumps along the way, but through the Holy Spirit's power and leading, you need not live a life of secret sin. Jesus demands all who profess faith in His name stop sinning. The truly saved will stop. Jesus' expectation for the born again believer contrasts with those who emphasize that believers will continue to sin daily in thought, word, and deed. Jesus tells us we do not have to sin.

I hear the excuses in your minds right now. Sin no more? Asking this man to sin no more seems like an impossible request, an intolerable burden, but it is actually part of the Good News. In the first place, it implies he has been forgiven. Here we see a redeeming Savior at work; He came to "take away the sins of the world." This gospel and John's later letters reveal a theme of being free from the power of sin. By healing him, Jesus was offering this man a new lease on life: to live free of the debilitation that had wrecked his life and his prospects. In essence, He offered him hope and power to move far beyond his own frailty and weakness, physical and spiritual. Here we see the Lamb of God at work, taking away the sins of the world, forgiving even those who would go on to betray him. But furthermore, there is a theme in John and 1 John that Christians have been freed from the power of sin. Jesus was challenging this man to a new life, the life from above The barest glimmer of faith on this man's part brought Jesus' healing to his life, and then he was to move far beyond both his physical and spiritual weakness.

Getting Free and Staying Free

God, grant me the serenity to accept the things I cannot change; courage to change the things I can; and the wisdom to know the difference. Amen.

Known to many as the *Serenity Prayer*, the words above offer a challenge to all who desire to have a closer walk with the Lord. It lets us know we have a responsibility for our actions and our commitment to becoming the person God ordained us to be. We are admonished to "change the things [we] can" rather than simply praying for God to do all the work. Many self-help groups like *Alcoholics Anonymous* use the *Serenity Prayer* as the healing mantra. It is oft repeated as a reminder of the continuous process of being freed from addictions of all sorts.

These same groups have developed Twelve Steps to Recovery plans that encourage those who seek freedom from addictive behaviors that are often personally destructive—not to mention their negative impact upon family members and others. These 12-step programs have been helpful to many men and women who have endeavored to find peace in their lives. These programs only offer recovery, but the Lord wants us—the servants, children, and friends of God—to be freed from addictive behaviors and any other thing that hinders our spiritual growth. Those who attend and participate in recovery programs continue to rehearse their pasts, no matter how long they have been clean and sober. They introduce themselves by their former habits. "Hello, I'm Brian, and I am an alcoholic."

Utilizing an adapted version of the AA recovery plans, this section will detail what I call the Spiritual Freedom Plan. Each step will offer sound spiritual advice and evidence from the Word of the Lord. Study the Scriptures; commit them to memory; use them in those tough times when the enemy of your soul throws those old behaviors and habits in your face. Remember the psalmist's advice: *"Thy word have I hid in mine heart, that I might not sin against thee"* (119:11).

Freedom Step	**Underlying Principle**	**Related Scriptures**
1. Admit you are powerless.	Without God's help, we are weak. Old habits die hard; they want to control you. Don't trust your own strength, character, or willpower.	Romans 7:18-20; Psalms 6:2,4
2. Believe in the one who has greater power and is able to restore you.	In your weakness, God shows His strength. The scriptures teach us to *"Be strong in the Lord and in the power of His might"* (Ephesians 6:10).	Mark 9:23-24; Luke 13:10-13; Psalm 142; Psalm 18:1-3

3. Make a decision to turn your will and life over to the care of God	He made you and knows all about you. He knows your weaknesses and your strengths. So, why not yield completely to Him?	Matthew 11:28-30; Matthew 16:26; 2 Chronicles 7:14; Proverbs 3:5-6
4. Search yourself.	We each must recognize the internal war between the flesh and the spirit. No one is impervious to the cull of sin as long as we are in this mortal body. We must be attuned to potential areas of weakness.	Romans 13:11-14; 1 Corinthians 11:28; Galatians 6:3-5; Proverbs 16:2-3; Luke 11:35
5. Admit to God, yourself and to another person the exact nature of your problem.	Secrecy is one of satan's greatest weapons. As long as you keep your problem hidden, he can use it against you. It's also much easier to fall into temptation when you're not accountable.	Luke 15:17-20; Acts 19:17-20; Hebrews 4:12-16; James 5:16
6. Be ready and open to allow God to remove all the defects of your character.	When you recognize you are weak—and that God is all-powerful—be ready for Him to reward you with more of His Spirit.	Romans 6:11-12; Ephesians 4:17-23; Revelation 3:19-20

7. Humbly ask God to forgive and remove your shortcomings.	The Lord is a masterful surgeon. Let Him give you a sinectomy before it is too late. It might hurt a little, but the solution is much better than the problem.	Matthew 18:4; Acts 3:19; Hebrews 12:5-11
8. Recognize you are not the only beneficiary of your problem.	There is no such thing as an individual sin. Your actions affect all those who come in contact with you, especially your spouse and children. And don't forget those who are watching your Christian witness.	Matthew 18:21-25; Exodus 34:6-8
9. Search yourself again with those to whom you are accountable.	Continue to look for patterns and themes that emerge. Ask your partners to help you identify areas for growth.	James 5:16
10. Pray to and meditate on God, praying for knowledge of His will and the power to do it.	The more you focus on God, the stronger you are in the fight for your soul.	Psalm 1; Galatians 2:20; Philippians 4:8, 13

11. Realize that God has set you free so you can carry the message to someone else who is bound.	As bad and embarrassing as the habit might be, someone else may be suffering and you might have the antidote. We overcome by the blood of the Lamb and the word of our testimony.	Mark 5:18-20; 1 Corinthians 9:22-27; 1 Timothy 1:12-16
12. Apply these principles to all areas of your life.	If it works for bad habits, it will work in any area of your life. Walk with the Lord, and He will walk with you.	1 Thessalonians 2:10-12; 3:12-13

You will note that each step and principle is connected to scriptural references. Many who write books about secret sin negate the power of the Word alone. The *sintimate* often recount the number of scriptures they have memorized, but memorization alone is not enough. The Scriptures help us identify changes we must make. The Word of God, if we let it, powerfully cuts and penetrates to the core of our being *"and is a discerner of the thoughts and intents of the heart"* (Hebrews 4:12). Applying the Scriptures, or clearly lining up our thoughts, activities, and interactions with others with the Word of God, becomes paramount.

CHAPTER FOUR
FROM DEATH TO LIFE

"Don't wash your garments in polluted water."—Rebekah Mitchell

This book is not designed to make you feel bad or guilty "no condemnation" (Romans 8:1) but to present to you the possibility of moving beyond your *sintimacy* (eradicating it is a better description). I hope you understand that there is a better way. There is healing and restoration, but so much of this is up to you. I heard an evangelist once say, "No matter how many steps you have taken backwards or away from God, it only takes one step towards Him." The Potter is ready to stick you back on the wheel; He can fix what is broken. Jesus is calling you to recommitment and surrender. You have tried it your way long enough. Your kids, your spouse, your church, your community all need you to be whole and in right standing with the Lord. They need you to rise from the dead. Sin can visit the third and fourth generations

(Exodus 20:5; 34:7; Number 14:18; Deuteronomy 5:9). Break the curse! Imagine your children, grandchildren and great grandchildren experiencing the same—if not worse—problems you have. You have the power to impact generations.

Jesus stood before his friend's tomb weeping and angry. John 11:33 reads, *"He groaned in the spirit and was troubled."* The Greek word for groaned suggests Jesus' anger was related to the misery caused by sin, satan, and death. Jesus informed the onlookers that they would see the glory of God (v. 40). Jesus was there to perform a miracle. In this single act, He would show His true power: the ability to give life when there is none, that death itself was no match for the Almighty Incarnate God. And He did it—with just a word.

I will be honest with you. To me, the real miracle was not performed by Jesus. Personally, the headliner of this story is Lazarus. Think about it. The dead man responded to Jesus. Standing there before the onlookers, Jesus had a conversation with his Father: "Lord, do this for them. They will believe you if they see this." His instructions were to remove the stone from the entrance to the tomb. "Lazarus, come forth. *And he that was dead came forth*" (v. 44, italics mine).

There are four things you need to realize about that moment:

1. Lazarus had been dead in the grave for four days.
2. He was bound from head to toe in the clothes of a dead man.
3. He could not see where he was going because his face was covered.
4. The tomb was just a hole in the wall, not a nice coffin or mausoleum; it was more likely just a hole large enough to slide the body into.

Though bound, blind and trapped in a hole, this man responded to the Lord's voice. Do you know why? Lazarus did not want to be dead anymore. On the first call, Lazarus got moving. He didn't say, "Hey, can somebody help me out of here?" He made no complaints that he could not see where he was going. He heard Jesus' voice and followed the simple instructions. No excuses. The directive was come and he came. So what will you do, *Sintimate* One? The Holy One has given the imperative, calling you back from the brink of spiritual death. How will you respond?

Only after Lazarus did his part did Jesus speak to those around to help him out of his bands. (This shows the importance of accountability relationships.) I can just imagine the joy in Lazarus' countenance when he saw the faces of those who had taken the napkin from his face and helped him out of his mummy suit.

With Christ's help and direction, you can be freed—and stay free. Let's talk about how to do that. The *sintimacy* needs to end. Scripture says that, when we live in sin, it's like we're nailing Jesus to the cross again. Why would we want to put Him through that agony again? I can't imagine the Father enjoys seeing His Son tortured like that time after time. In fact, it makes Him angry. Look at these verses from Colossians 3:5-10, 24-25:

> *"So put to death the sinful, earthly things lurking within you. Have nothing to do with sexual immorality, impurity, lust, and evil desires. Don't be greedy, for a greedy person is an idolater, worshiping the things of this world.* ***Because of these sins, the anger of God is coming****. You used to do these things when your life was still part of this world. But now is the time to get rid of anger, rage, malicious behavior, slander, and dirty language. Don't lie to each other,* ***for you have stripped off your old sinful nature and all its wicked deeds. Put on your new nature, and be renewed as you learn to know your Creator and become like him****...Remember that the Lord will give you an inheritance as your reward, and that the Master you are serving is Christ.* ***But if you do what is wrong, you***

> ***will be paid back for the wrong you have done****. For God has no favorites."*

Don't you just love the fact that the Almighty gives us options? You do have a choice: Live for God and experience His presence, newness of life, and His protection or live for yourself (and satan) and you take your chances against His wrath. It really seems like an easy decision. Make the choice to live your life God's way rather than your own.

To stay free from *sintimacy*, we must actively wage war against the forces of darkness in our lives. We cannot afford to be passive. Yes, we have the victory through Christ's redemption, but we should be on the offensive in spiritual warfare. In his letter to Timothy, Paul put it this way: *"Let everyone that nameth the name of Christ depart from iniquity"* (2 Timothy 2:19). If you say you belong to God, then you are no longer your own. If you call Jesus "Lord," you must acknowledge His ownership.

◇◇

"To stay free from sintimacy, we must actively wage war against the forces of darkness."

◇◇

I can hear you now: "Yeah, that's easier said than done." If you're like I was when I was caught up in my life of secret sin, the guilt and shame are overwhelming. I always felt like I was the worst person ever and that it would take a miracle to see true freedom. So, let's start right where you are. First, you have to want to be free and you have to believe Jesus can make the difference (Hebrews 11:6). Second, you must get out of the cursed place, if you expect to see the miracle. In Mark 8:22-26, Jesus was traveling through Bethsaida and a blind man was brought to Him for healing. Jesus took the man by the hand and led him out of town and then spit on his eyes and laid His hands on the man to receive sight.

Doesn't it seem peculiar that Jesus led the man out of the village? Most of His miracles were instantaneous, on-the-spot occurrences, but this required something different. You see, Bethsaida was under the curse of judgment for their lack of repentance (hint, hint). In Matthew's gospel, Jesus quite sternly spoke to the people of Bethsaida and the surrounding areas:

> *"What horrors await you, Korazin and Bethsaida! For if the miracles I did in you had been done in wicked Tyre and Sidon, their people would have sat in deep repentance long ago, clothed in sackcloth and throwing ashes on their heads to show their remorse. I assure you, Tyre and Sidon will be better off on the judgment day than you! And you people of Capernaum, will you be exalted to heaven? No, you will be brought down to the place of the dead. For if the miracles I did for you had been done in Sodom, it would still be here today. I assure you, Sodom will be better off on the judgment day than you"* (Matthew 11:21-22).

No wonder Jesus chose to remove this man from Bethsaida.

When Jesus removed His hands from the man's eyes, He asked him if he was able to see. The man admitted he could, but not clearly. His eyes were still a bit dim. He acknowledged everything was not all right. One of the biggest reasons we do not get totally free is that we often do not admit we are still wrestling with certain things. We want free from the big stuff, but deny the existence of the "little foxes" or forget to acknowledge the multiple layers of sin. For instance, my addiction to pornography was not the only problem. There were usually multiple layers that needed to be repented of: reading the magazines or visiting inappropriate sites on the

Internet; masturbating; adultery (scripture says that it's the thought that counts); lying to my wife about what I was doing or where I had been; an out-of-control fantasy life that cheated my wife of my full sexual attention and focus. Need I go on?

This story in Mark is the only instance of Jesus performing a gradual miracle. After the blind man acknowledged he still did not see clearly, Jesus again covered his eyes. This time He turned the man's eyes toward heaven. In that act of looking up, the man's sight was completely restored. The man's positioning and view of God had to change to aright his condition. He had to leave the place of cursing and then fix his gaze upon God, the One who could give him freedom. Notice that Jesus forbade him from ever returning to Bethsaida. He was not even to share the news of his deliverance with anyone from the village. This means we should completely sever the ties with our past lives if we desire to stay free. Make the decision. As human beings, there is truly only one surety, and that is the ever-present reality of death. Jesus can bring us to life, but we must live so we do not enter death again.

How to Stay Clean and Free

I know I promised no simple steps, but for the sake of argument, I will let you know some ways to stay alive and not remain dead in sin.

Step 1: New Life in Christ

Your relationship with Christ should change your behavior. You were made free to walk in newness of life. When I counsel parents who are having difficulties with their teenagers or younger children, I often talk to them about teaching the children to see alternatives to their behaviors. As parents, one of the first things we say to our children is no. Think about it. When your child first started toddling around and went near the hot stove or touched the electrical outlet, you probably yelled, "No!" You scolded and possibly, spanked the child. What we often fail to do, however, is give the child something that is OK to touch instead. Thankfully, the Scriptures don't leave us hanging like that.

In the fourth chapter of his letter to the Ephesians, the apostle Paul admonished the Christians who had *"learned the truth that is in Jesus"* to *"throw off your old evil nature and your former way of life, which is rotten through and through, full of lust and deception"*(vs. 23). He could have stopped there; those are really good instructions. Ostensibly, what he said was "Now that you know Christ, stop doing the things you used to do; that's not you anymore" (vs. 24).

Step 2: Dead to Sin

In acknowledging Christ as Savior and Redeemer, I recognize His power to kill the effects of sin in my life. In fact, when I share in His resurrection (through water baptism), the old ways are made powerless (Romans 6:6). Through the power of His resurrection, our slavery to sin has been destroyed (2 Corinthians 5:17; Ephesians 4:22; Colossians 3:9-10) and we can faithfully weed out the fruit of sin in our lives (Titus 2:11-14). We do this by denying ourselves (self-control); refusing to allow our physical bodies to become "instruments of unrighteousness" (Romans 6:13); through spiritual warfare that includes fasting (self denial); and consistent prayer (1 Corinthians 7:5; Matthew 17:20-22).

Step 3: Come Out of the Grave

Jesus commanded the stone be rolled away and called the dead to come forth. There is no stone except for what you replace it with. In other words, the only thing stopping you is you. After accepting Christ, we must continue to choose whom we will serve. If you cease to oppose sin's domination, you can easily become enslaved again—and you know the potential results. Or, you can be free and continue to be transformed into "servants to righteousness unto holiness" (Romans 6:19).

Step 4: Change Your Clothes

Jesus told the disciples to "loose Lazarus and let him go." Lazarus could have decided to keep his mummified suit on, but I imagine he didn't like the stink of the grave on him. I wonder how much we like the funk that is in our old clothes.

Step 5: Submit to a New Authority, a New Headship

Romans 6:12 is a terrific reminder of our responsibility to change masters. Stop right now and repeat this scripture at least five times: *"Let not sin therefore reign in your mortal body, that ye should obey it in the lusts thereof."* Remember, this walk is about ownership and dominion. You must dethrone the enemy's influence in your life: mentally, physically, emotionally, and spiritually.

Step 6: Give Up Control

On my first day of working at a particular job, my former boss sat me down and said this: "In order to gain control, you need to give it up." Read Colossians 3. This chapter is parallel to Ephesians 5. Both chapters deal with issues of submission. They talk about the roles of husbands, wives, and children. We often use these scriptures as doctrinal statements, but we miss some of the intent. Ephesians 5 talks about living in and being submitted to the Spirit of God. In Colossians 3, the emphasis is on being filled with the Word of God. When the Word controls your life, you will be joyful, thankful, and submissive, and these are the same characteristics of the Spirit-filled Christian as explained in Ephesians 5.

To be filled with the Spirit of God means to be controlled by the Word of God. What we are speaking of here is the wonderful regeneration provided by new birth in Christ. Regeneration comes to those whose hearts are turned towards the Lord in sincere repentance, who no longer conform to the patterns of this world, and whose faith is centered on Christ. This is necessary because our natural selves are incapable of pleasing God. We need to be transformed into a vessel of honor to serve the King. This regeneration involves transitioning from the old life and former self to a new life of complete obedience to Christ. The regenerated are set free from the authority of sin, and their new spirit seeks to line up with the expressed will of God.

A regenerated person cannot, and will not, make habitual sin a practice. In fact, 1 John 3:9 and 1:5-7 contend that we cannot maintain a connection to the Father without sincerely turning from sin. We have been given the grace that overcomes the influences of the world through a sustained relationship with Christ and the indwelling Holy Spirit. Continuing to live in sin can snuff out the light and life of Christ in a believer. Put succinctly, *"If ye live after the flesh, ye shall die"* (Romans 8:13).

Always remember that our membership as citizens of the kingdom of God is conditionally based upon our faith, obedience and love (Romans 8:12-14; 2 Timothy 2:12).

Chapter Five
Applying Scriptures

"For the word of God is quick, and powerful, and sharper than any two-edged sword, piercing even to the dividing asunder of soul and spirit, and of the joints and marrow, and is a discerner of the thoughts and intents of the heart" (Hebrews 4:12).

As I have mentioned multiples times throughout this book, it is so important for you to recognize the power of the Word of God as the only way out of *sintimacy*. David said it best: *"Thy Word have I hidden in my heart that I might not sin..."* Appropriately applying the Scriptures is essential. If you need a healer, the best bet is to use the scriptures that apply to healing. Isaiah 55:11 reveals that God's Word will not return to Him void, which means it will accomplish its intended purpose. We can speak specifically to our struggles with the overcoming power of the Word.

When I finally made up my mind that I was done with living for my *sintimacy* of pornography, the Lord directed me to read, study, and ruminate on 1 Thessalonians 4:1-7:

> *"Furthermore then we beseech you, brethren, and exhort you by the Lord Jesus, that as ye have received of us how ye ought to walk and to please God, so ye would abound more and more. For ye know what commandments we gave you by the Lord Jesus. For this is the will of God, even your sanctification, that ye should abstain from fornication: That every one of you should know how to possess his vessel in sanctification and honour; Not in the lust of concupiscence, even as the Gentiles which know not God: That no man go beyond and defraud his brother in any matter: because that the Lord is the avenger of all such, as we also have forewarned you and testified. For God hath not called us unto uncleanness, but unto holiness."*

This scripture became my best friend. I recited it to myself at least four times a day. In the time of temptation, I would focus on the part about possessing my vessel in sanctification and honor. I had to learn how to control and manage my body in order to maintain my purity and consecration from the profane. It became life to me. The more I recited it, the more I believed. The more I believed, the stronger I became. The stronger I became, the more I could stand firm in my liberty. There were certainly other scriptures that dealt with my particular problem, and I also studied them, but this one spoke to what I wanted to become: a vessel of honor.

In this final chapter, I have taken the liberty of pointing to general scriptures that relate to *sintimacy*, freedom, rewards and consequences (better expressed as blessings and judgment), and the function of God's Spirit in our lives. Additionally, you will find scriptures that speak specifically to common *sintimate* behaviors. It is not an exhaustive list by any means, but you can also search the Scriptures for yourself. Through the Word, examine yourself. Use it as a means of self-inspection. Like a masterful surgeon, the Word can get to the deepest part of our nature—even to the hidden things. It cuts us open to begin the healing process. Our thoughts are laid bare, our motives exposed and our excuses obliterated.

Combatting Sintimacy

To effectively obtain your freedom, you are being asked to commit the following scriptures to memory. Study them daily.

Romans 6:4-19

"Therefore we are buried with him by baptism into death: that like as Christ was raised up from the dead by the glory of the Father, even so ***we also should walk in newness of life.*** *For if we have been planted together in the likeness of his death, we shall be also in the* ***likeness of his resurrection****:* *[6]Knowing this, that our* ***old man is crucified with him,*** *that the body of sin might be destroyed, that henceforth* ***we should not serve sin****.* ***For he that is dead is freed from sin.*** *Now if we be dead with Christ, we believe that we shall also live with him: Knowing that Christ being raised from the dead dieth no more; death hath no more dominion over him. For in that he died, he died unto sin once: but in that he liveth, he* ***liveth unto God****. Likewise reckon ye also yourselves to be* ***dead indeed unto sin, but alive unto God through Jesus Christ our Lord. Let not sin therefore reign*** *in your mortal body, that ye should obey it in the lusts thereof. Neither yield ye your members as instruments of unrighteousness unto sin: but* ***yield yourselves unto God****, as those that are alive from the dead, and your members as* ***instruments of righteousness*** *unto God.* ***For sin shall not have dominion over you****: for ye are not under the law, but under grace. What then? shall we sin, because we are not under the law, but under grace? God forbid. Know ye not, that to whom ye yield yourselves servants to obey, his servants ye are to whom ye obey; whether of sin unto death, or*

of obedience unto righteousness? ***But God be thanked, that ye were the servants of sin****, but ye have obeyed from the heart that form of doctrine which was delivered you. Being then made free from sin, ye became the* ***servants of righteousness. I speak after the manner of men because of the infirmity of your flesh: for as ye have yielded your members servants to uncleanness and to iniquity unto iniquity; even so now yield your members servants to righteousness unto holiness"*** (NLT).

Romans 12:1-2

"And so, dear brothers and sisters, I plead with you to give your bodies to God. Let them be a living and holy sacrifice—the kind he will accept. When you think of what he has done for you, is this too much to ask? Don't copy the behavior and customs of this world, but let God transform you into a new person by changing the way you think. Then you will know what God wants you to do, and you will know how good and pleasing and perfect his will really is" (NLT).

Hebrews 12: 1

"Therefore, since we are surrounded by such a huge crowd of witnesses to the life of faith, let us strip off every weight that slows us down, especially the sin that so easily hinders our progress. And let us run with endurance the race that God has set before us" (NLT).

Colossians 3:1-17

"Since you have been raised to new life with Christ, set your sights on the realities of heaven, where Christ sits at God's right hand in the place of honor and power. Let heaven fill your thoughts. Do not think only about things down here on earth. For you died when Christ died, and your real life is hidden with Christ in God. And when Christ, who is your real life, is revealed to the whole world, you will share in all his glory. ***So put to death the sinful, earthly things lurking within you****. Have nothing to do with sexual sin, impurity, lust, and shameful desires. Don't be greedy for the good things of this life, for that is idolatry. God's terrible anger will*

come upon those who do such things. ***You used to do them when your life was still part of this world. But now is the time*** *to get rid of anger, rage, malicious behavior, slander, and dirty language. Don't lie to each other, for* ***you have stripped off your old evil nature and all its wicked deeds. In its place you have clothed yourselves with a brand-new nature that is continually being renewed as you learn more and more about Christ, who created this new nature within you****. In this new life, it doesn't matter if you are a Jew or a Gentile, circumcised or uncircumcised, barbaric, uncivilized, slave, or free.* ***Christ is all that matters****, and he lives in all of us. Since God chose you to be the holy people whom he loves, you must clothe* ***yourselves*** *with tenderhearted mercy, kindness, humility, gentleness, and patience. You must make allowance for each other's faults and forgive the person who offends you.* ***Remember, the Lord forgave you****, so you must forgive others. And the most important piece of clothing you must wear is love. Love is what binds us all together in perfect harmony. And* ***let the peace that comes from Christ rule in your hearts****. For as members of one body you are all called to live in peace. And always be thankful.* ***Let the words of Christ****, in all their richness, live in your hearts and make you wise. Use his words to teach and counsel each other. Sing psalms and hymns and spiritual songs to God with thankful hearts. And whatever you do or say, let it be as a representative of the Lord Jesus, all the while giving thanks through him to God the Father"* (NLT).

2 Corinthians 5:17

"Therefore if any man be in Christ, he is a new creature: old things are passed away; behold, all things are become new."

2 Corinthians 6:17-18

"Wherefore come out from among them, and be ye separate, saith the Lord, and touch not the unclean thing; and I will receive you. And will be a Father unto you, and ye shall be my sons and daughters, saith the Lord Almighty."

"Therefore, come out from among unbelievers, and separate yourselves from them, says the Lord. Don't touch their filthy things, and I will welcome you. And I will be your Father, and you will be my sons and daughters, says the Lord Almighty" (NLT).

Romans 6:11-22

"Likewise reckon ye also yourselves to be dead indeed unto sin, but alive unto God through Jesus Christ our Lord. Let not sin therefore reign in your mortal body, that ye should obey it in the lusts thereof. Neither yield ye your members as instruments of unrighteousness unto sin: but yield yourselves unto God, as those that are alive from the dead, and your members as instruments of righteousness unto God. For sin shall not have dominion over you: for ye are not under the law, but under grace. What then? shall we sin, because we are not under the law, but under grace? God forbid. Know ye not, that to whom ye yield yourselves servants to obey, his servants ye are to whom ye obey; whether of sin unto death, or of obedience unto righteousness? But God be thanked, that ye were the servants of sin, but ye have obeyed from the heart that form of doctrine which was delivered you. Being then made free from sin, ye became the servants of righteousness. I speak after the manner of men because of the infirmity of your flesh: for as ye have yielded your members servants to uncleanness and to iniquity unto iniquity; even so now yield your members servants to righteousness unto holiness. For when ye were the servants of sin, ye were free from righteousness. What fruit had ye then in those things whereof ye are now ashamed? for the end of those things is death. But now being made free from sin, and become servants to God, ye have your fruit unto holiness, and the end everlasting life."

"So you also should consider yourselves to be dead to the power of sin and alive to God through Christ Jesus. Do not let sin control the way you live, do not give in to sinful desires. Do not let any part of your body become an instrument of evil to serve sin. Instead, give yourselves completely to God,

for you were dead, but now you have new life. So use your whole body as an instrument to do what is right for the glory of God. Sin is no longer your master, for you no longer live under the requirements of the law. Instead, you live under the freedom of God's grace. Well then, since God's grace has set us free from the law, does that mean we can go on sinning? Of course not! Don't you realize that you become the slave of whatever you choose to obey? You can be a slave to sin, which leads to death, or you can choose to obey God, which leads to righteous living. Thank God! Once you were slaves of sin, but now you wholeheartedly obey this teaching we have given you. Now you are free from your slavery to sin, and you have become slaves to righteous living. Because of the weakness of your human nature, I am using the illustration of slavery to help you understand all this. Previously, you let yourselves be slaves to impurity and lawlessness, which led ever deeper into sin. Now you must give yourselves to be slaves to righteous living so that you will become holy. When you were slaves to sin, you were free from the obligation to do right. And what was the result? You are now ashamed of the things you used to do, things that end in eternal doom. But now you are free from the power of sin and have become slaves of God. Now you do those things that lead to holiness and result in eternal life" (NLT).

Philipians 4:8

"Finally, brethren, whatsoever things are true, whatsoever things are honest, whatsoever things are just, whatsoever things are pure, whatsoever things are lovely, whatsoever things are of good report; if there be any virtue, and if there be any praise, think on these things."

"And now, dear brothers and sisters, one final thing. Fix your thoughts on what is true, and honorable, and right, and pure, and lovely, and admirable. Think about things that are excellent and worthy of praise" (NLT).

Romans 8:13

"For if ye live after the flesh, ye shall die: but if ye through the Spirit do

mortify the deeds of the body, ye shall live."

"For if you live by its dictates, you will die. But if through the power of the Spirit you put to death the deeds of your sinful nature, you will live" (NLT).

1 John 3:8-10
"He that committeth sin is of the devil; for the devil sinneth from the beginning. For this purpose the Son of God was manifested, that he might destroy the works of the devil. Whosoever is born of God doth not commit sin; for his seed remaineth in him: and he cannot sin, because he is born of God. In this the children of God are manifest, and the children of the devil: whosoever doeth not righteousness is not of God, neither he that loveth not his brother."

"But when people keep on sinning, it shows that they belong to the devil, who has been sinning since the beginning. But the Son of God came to destroy the works of the devil. Those who have been born into God's family do not make a practice of sinning, because God's life is in them. So they can't keep on sinning, because they are children of God. So now we can tell who are children of God and who are children of the devil. Anyone who does not live righteously and does not love other believers does not belong to God" (NLT).

2 Peter 2:9-10
"So you see, the Lord knows how to rescue godly people from their trials, even while punishing the wicked right up until the day of judgment. He is especially hard on those who follow their own evil, lustful desires and who despise authority. These people are proud and arrogant, daring even to scoff at the glorious ones without so much as trembling."

Some passages to memorize when facing temptation:

Immorality: Romans 13:14

Lying: John 8:44; Colossians 3:9

Gossiping: James 4:11

Disobeying Parents: Hebrews 3:17

Discouragement: Galatians 6:9

Fear of the Future: 2 Timothy 1:7

Lust: Matthew 5:28; 2 Timothy 2:22

Desire for Revenge: Matthew 6:15

Neglect of God's Word: Matthew 4:4

Worry over Finances: Matthew 6:24-34; Philippians 4:6

Epilogue

Moving Beyond Failure

Around the country, there are news stories of yet another Christian leader who has fallen from grace. Another family in distress. Another church in stunned disarray, scrambling to pick up the pieces. Thankfully, life goes on and healing takes place for the most part, but I often wonder about that poor soul who was at the heart of all the hullabaloo. Why? Because, frankly, that should have been me. For all intents and purposes, I should have been "found out." My dirty little secret should have been, could have been, might have been slathered over the front pages of the local newspaper. Thanks to the mercy and grace of God, it was not. I had the chance to tell on myself, receive appropriate and loving redirection, and get back in line with the will of God.

Like John Edwards, no one can beat me up more than I already have. I will go to my grave with thoughts of my life of repeated failure ringing in my ears. Although it has been several years since I left the darkness of secret sin, I still have recurring memories that get me down from time to time. How could I have been so selfish and stupid? How could I have risked so much: my family, my position in the church, the parishioners who looked to me for counsel and leadership?

I want to conclude this book with some encouragement to you, the one who is looking for freedom. There is another side to this story—to your story. You need not stay lost. Our God is passionate about you and wants to restore you to your original glory in Him. He still has a work for you to do. It may have shifted or it could be the very same message. God has given each of His children an assignment, something to be accomplished for His kingdom, something you specifically have been given to do. In fact, He specializes in redeeming the wayward soul. King David is a great example. He failed God in multiple ways, but David lived so that the Son of God would be born through his lineage. Some of the most profound poetry, songs, prayers, and scriptures that we quote today came from his quill. Theologians and secular scholars examine and teach his words as some of the most eloquent and dramatic literature since antiquity.

There are others. Four names in particular come to mind: Adam, Moses, Jonah, and Peter. Each had been given a particular assignment. God had chosen these men to do something special for Him. Each failed. Each failure had repercussions. For most of them, however, God restored and put them right back on the mission field. Let's look at them for a moment.

ADAM

Given two things by God: an assignment (be a steward over God's creation) and dominion

His failure was forgetting who he was and loving Eve more than God.

His failure caused the fall of man.

MOSES

His assignment was to use what was in his hand.

His past could have haunted him. He was an abandoned baby who became an adopted prince who became a murderer who became a fugitive who became a shepherd who became the savior of his people.

His failure was making excuses and acting out in anger. His failure cost him his inheritance.

His salvation was in the fact that he surrendered the tools of his trade to the Lord's power.

JONAH

Like Adam, he was given an assignment: preach repentance to the nation of Nineveh.

His failures were running away and unforgiveness. His failure almost caused the death of his shipmates, and ultimately he became whale vomit. Although he failed, his assignment never changed.

His salvation was in the fact that he became obedient and a people were saved.

PETER

He was given the keys of the kingdom.

His failure was fear that led to his denial of Christ. His failure cost Christ His life. His failure caused him to run back to his old life.

Christ gave him the opportunity to redeem himself. His redemption brought about the beginning of the 1st century church.

Peter's story is an interesting one on which to conclude. He was one of the personally chosen, handpicked men of Christ himself. Chosen for his dexterity and deep convictions, Peter was a hothead, but he loved his

Christ. He told Jesus he would walk over hot coals, over broken shards of glass, through molten lava rather than be separated from him. When the soldiers came for Jesus in the Garden, it was Peter who drew the sword and chopped off Malchus' ear. But Jesus had already warned Peter that very evening, "Before the morning alarm, you will deny me three times." Peter was incredulous. "It's me, Jesus. Cephas/Peter—the one whom you prophesied the church would be built upon. You called me the Rock. How can you say that I will deny you. Never, not me. Uh uh!" When that cock crowed the third time, Peter must have felt like stir-fried pond scum. Peter had, in fact, denied even knowing Jesus, acting as if he had never even met Him before. Twelve hours later, Jesus was dead. Talk about failure!

When we next see Peter, he had "left the church" and went back to his boat. Moments later, the resurrected Christ was standing before him and some of the other disciples. They had been unsuccessfully fishing all night long.

Jesus looked directly into Peter's eyes and asked him an all-important question: "Peter, do you love me?"

Peter responded, "Of course I love you, Jesus."

Jesus reminded Peter of his assigned responsibility. "Then feed my sheep." This exchange happened three times. Three times Jesus asked Peter if he loved Him; three Peter affirmed his love; and three times Jesus gave Peter an assignment. This is significant. Peter had failed Jesus three times. He had denied him three times. And here is the mercy and grace of God: Jesus gave Peter the opportunity to make it right. In those precious moments before His ascension, Jesus fully restored Peter to his place as an apostle, and Peter went on to be a phenomenon for the kingdom. The church would not be "the Church" had it not been for Peter.

And so, here you are. You may have failed Jesus multiple times. Yet, you still have a job to do. Someone is waiting for you to minister to them, to present Christ to them, to bring them to a place of repentance or deliverance (Luke 4:19-20). Your assignment has not changed. Jesus wants to restore you. His expectations for you are high, and He is giving you a chance to redeem yourself, to make your word good to Him, to prove to Him that you are chasing after His heart. You have the opportunity, right here and now, to break the curse, to shake off the bonds and shackles of persistent sin. Right now, you are at the base of Mount Sinai with the many others who have forgotten how God delivered them and set them free from bondage. Millions had decided to bare themselves in worship before a handmade idol, and a shocked Moses stood before them asking, "Who is on the Lord's side?" You can be like Levi, who for years had borne the curse of his past mistakes (Genesis 49), and take that step and say, "I am" (Exodus 32:25-27).

At the time of his prophetic ministry, Isaiah had to give some pretty strong messages to an apostate Israel. But two particular prophetic utterances spoke of Israel's restoration and return from exile. In verses one and two of the fortieth chapter, Isaiah tells her that she is forgiven, that the nation had been punished long enough. Their God was returning to them. Oh what joy must have filled the houses and the temple! You, too, can hear these words when you fully repent and turn from your *sintimate* ways. Hear, in this second message, the Spirit of the Lord speaking to you through the prophet Isaiah. He is making Himself known to you, letting you know your value to Him.

> *"Regarding Zion, I can't keep my mouth shut, regarding Jerusalem, I can't hold my tongue, Until her righteousness blazes down like the sun and her salvation flames up like a torch. Foreign countries will see your righteousness, and world leaders your glory.* ***You'll*** *get a* ***brand-new name*** *straight from the mouth of God. You'll be a stunning crown in the palm of God's hand, a jeweled gold cup held high*

> *in the hand of your God.* ***No more will anyone call you Rejected****, and your country will no more be called Ruined. You'll be called Hephzibah (My Delight), and your land Beulah (Married), Because God delights in you and your land will be like a wedding celebration. For as a young man marries his virgin bride, so your builder marries you, And as a bridegroom is happy in his bride, so your God is happy with you"* (Isaiah 62:1-5 *The Message*).

Right now, you may feel that you are at the edge of His Mercy. That's how most of us feel: like we're too far away for God to even care anymore. But these are the lies the devil wants us to believe. If you have cared enough to read this book, there is hope. There is always hope. And God gives us this hope and faith to find our way back to Him. You can do it! God delivered me, and I have faith to know He can deliver you and your loved ones also.

endnotes

1. Carver, George Washington, "Classic Quotes." The Quotations Page. 6 August 2009. <http://www.quotationspage.com/search.php3?homesearch=excuses>

2. Dictionary. "The American Heritage® Dictionary of the English Language," Fourth Edition Copyright © 2007, 2000 by Houghton Mifflin Company. Updated in 2007. 6 August 2009 <http://www.answers.com/Outdoor&r=67>

3. Scott, Sir Walter, "Marmion, Canto vi Stanza 17." The Quotations Page. 6 August 2009. <http://www.quotationspage.com/quote/27150.html>

4. Unknown, "Secret." Merriam-Webster Online Dictionary. 2009. Merriam-Webster Online. 6 August 2009. <http://www.merriam-webster.com/dictionary/secret>

5. Ibid.

6. Edwards, Sen. John, "Edwards Statement on Affair." CNN.com, 2008. CNN. 6 August 2009 <http://www.cnn.com/2008/POLITICS/08/08/edwards.statement/index.html?eref=rss_latest>

7. Henry, Matthew, "Elijah's Trial of the False Prophets." Bible Gateway. Public domain. Bible Gateway. 6 August 2009. <http://www.biblegateway.com/resources/commentaries/index.php?action=getCommentaryText&cid=28&source=2&seq=i.11.18.3&interface=print>

8. Meakin, John, "How to Overcome Sin." The Good News. 1997. The Good News. 6 August 2009. <http://www.gnmagazine.org/issues/gn09/overcomesin.htm>

9. Unknown, "Sanctify." Merriam-Webster Online Dictionary. 2009. Merriam-Webster Online. 6 August 2009. <http://www.merriam-webster.com/dictionary/sanctify>

10. Christy, Robert, "Proverbs, Maxims and Phrases of All Ages." Quoteland.com. 1888. Quoteland. 6 August 2009.<http://www.quoteland.com/author.asp?AUTHOR_ID=652>

11. Meurier, Gabriel. "Trésor des sentences." Welcome to the Quote Garden. Quote Garden. 6 August 2009.< http://www.quotegarden.com/excuses.html>

12. Haggard, Ted, "Ted Haggard: I Am a Deceiver and a Liar." Beliefnet.com. 2006. Beliefnet. 6 August 2009. <http://www.beliefnet.com/News/2006/11/Ted-Haggard-I-Am-A-Deceiver-And-A-Liar.aspx>

13. Unknown, "New Life Church Statement on Church's Investigation and Pastor Ted Haggard." Christian News Wire. 2006. Christian News Wire. 6 August 2009. <http://www.christiannewswire.com/news/679621431.html>

14. Haggard, Ted, "Ted Haggard: I Am a Deceiver and a Liar." Beliefnet.

com. 2006. Beliefnet. 6 August 2009. <http://www.beliefnet.com/News/2006/11/Ted-Haggard-I-Am-A-Deceiver-And-A-Liar.aspx>

15. Edwards, Sen. John, "Edwards Statement on Affair." CNN.com, 2008. CNN. 6 August 2009 <http://www.cnn.com/2008/POLITICS/08/08/edwards.statement/index.html?eref=rss_latest>

Breinigsville, PA USA
17 August 2009
222374BV00004B/2/P

9 781926 625300

CONTRASTING PLANS

Selwyn R. Stevens, Ph.D.

Published by

 Additional copies of this book are available from many bookstores, libraries, or from:

Jubilee Resources International Inc.
PO Box 3, Feilding 4740, New Zealand

or our secure Internet Webshop at
www.jubileeresources.org

ISBN 978-1-0670303-7-7

The author uses American English spelling, not the Queen's English.

Part 1 was originally published under the title "Have You & Your Family Been Hoodwinked by THE PLAN?" in 2019
Part 2 is the text of a sermon/teaching I did recently.
Appendix 1 was originally published under the title "This Gospel of the Kingdom" in 2010.
Appendix 2 was originally published as "Christian Baptisms" in 1991 & 2014.
Appendix 3 was also published as an article entitled "How to Reverse the Curse on Your Wealth" in 2023.

Your guarantee of accurate Information: various sources and authorities have been quoted in good faith throughout this book. Every attempt has been made to ensure these quotations are accurate and in context.

This book is dedicated to the Saints of God who toil to bring the light of the Gospel of Jesus Christ to people ensnared in the spiritual darkness and deception of secret societies, cults and occultism.

The author wishes to acknowledge and thank many people too numerous to mention here who have given advice and encouragement to put this message into print. Your prayer and support have been most valuable, and God's reward awaits you.

Introduction

Most people who read this will be Christians who are concerned about the way the world seems to be going, and asking what will their children and grandchildren be left with. Others who may read this may be people without a Christian faith, but they, too, are concerned about where things seem headed.

Recently I was asked to address a conference, and while praying and contemplating what God would have me share, He indicated for me to bring these two Plans for mankind into one message. God has always had His plan for mankind; and there have been many attempts over the millennia by those opposing God to develop an alternative. The first recorded attempt was by Nimrod and Semiramis as recorded in Genesis chapter 11.

In Part One I wish to outline the counterfeit plan that was developed by a Daughter of Perdition, Alice Ann Bailey.

In Part Two I want to unpack what our Savior and Lord Jesus Christ outlined for His followers to be doing, until He returns. Jesus proclaimed, **"This gospel of the Kingdom shall be preached in the whole world for a witness to all nations, and then the end shall come" (Matthew 24:14).** But very few Christians ever speak about His Kingdom.

It seems to me most Christian activity has fallen far short of what God requires. Many claim God's people lack the power to do what's required, which is why I sensed I should include three appendices here to address those issues.

In the first appendix, I explain the difference between the Gospel of the Kingdom that Jesus preached and commanded us to do the same, whereas many use the "Four Spiritual Laws" or the "Roman Road" to share what they think is the Gospel.

The second appendix explains why people need to be baptized in a way consistent with God's Word. Many people sitting in pews, some for decades, still need to obey Jesus on this issue too. There

is much spiritual freedom and empowerment that comes to a person who obeys God on this vital issue.

The third appendix explains a Biblically effective way to pray so we can have our needs met and be generous to God's work. *(It's not about the money, it's about proving God's Word true with your circumstances improving as a consequence.)*

For decades in my lifetime, and much longer for the Christian faith, there has been too much emphasis on religion instead of God's Kingdom. To quote Dr. Robert Farrar Capon, *"Christianity is not a religion. Christianity is the proclamation of the end of religion, not of a new religion, or even of the best of all religions... If the cross is the sign of anything, it's the sign that God has gone out of the religion business and solved all the world's problems without requiring a single human being to do a single religious thing. What the cross is actually a sign of is the fact that religion can't do a thing about the world's problems – that it never did work and it never will."* This realization is essential to grasp before we can move forward.

When Jesus returns, He will fully establish His Kingdom on the Earth. That simply means that everything not part of His Kingdom will not survive. It's crucial that your name is listed in His Book of Life for a starter. If it's not, I suggest you attend to that immediately, today! Then go and share this Gospel of His Kingdom with whoever the Lord tells you to.

Part One

THE PLAN

BY A DAUGHTER OF PERDITION

Let's clear the Clutter first:

Let us join and pray this:

Dear Heavenly Father: I Come To You In The Name Of The Lord Jesus Christ. And I Renounce And Turn From All Lies, All Preconceptions, Deceptions, And Self-deceptions, And All Unteachableness That I Or My Ancestors Have Believed Or Entertained.

I confess them as my sins and I ask to be cleansed from them by the Blood of the Lord Jesus Christ. I renounce all vows of secrecy and silence about all ungodly activities.

I command every lying spirit, and every spirit of deception, self-deception, and unteachableness, and any other spirits associated with these sins to leave me now, harmlessly on my natural breathing, and not to return to me or to anyone whom I love, in the Name of the Lord Jesus Christ.

In the name of the Lord Jesus Christ, I come out of agreement with and renounce all shame, blame and guilt, all fear, all fear of failure, all fear of rejection, all fear of men, all fear of offending and ridicule, and all fear of not hearing God.

Lord Jesus, you are the Truth, and I surrender all these areas to Your Holy Spirit, Who is the Spirit of Truth, and whom You promised would lead me into all truth. In Jesus' Name. Amen

During the 1990s I taught on the New Age in various places in my country. That teaching was put into book form in 1992 entitled ***"The New Age: The Old Lie in a New Package."***

This was followed a while later with another small book, ***"Unmasking Spiritualism: Supernatural Deceivers."***

My attitude has always been that of Abraham Lincoln, who said, *"I am not concerned as to whether God is on my side. What concerns me is, am I on God's side, for God is always right."*

I explained the New Age hopes, goals and beliefs were:

A One-World religion, a One-World government; personal happiness above all; that sin is obsolete; we need to learn how to tap into forces, or energy within us; evolution; reincarnation; that we need enlightenment, not salvation; and that there are no absolutes.

According to the Oxford Dictionary, The New Age is *"a set of beliefs intended to replace traditional western culture, with alternative approaches to religion, medicine, the environment, music, etc."*

At that time I listed the following New Age/Occultic Prophets/Writers as:

Emmanuel Swedenborg
Helena Petrovna Blavatsky
Alice Bailey
George Gurdjieff
P.D. Ouspensky
Edgar Cayce
Jeanne Dixon
Rudolf Steiner
William Branham
Maitreya/Bejamin Crème
Matthew Fox
Napoleon Hill
Shirley MacLaine
Norman Vincent Peale
Paul Foster Case
Buckminster Fuller
Elizabeth Kubler-Ross
Sathya Sai Baba
Ram Dass

In response to their writings, I remind Christians of Paul's writing: **"Beware lest anyone cheat you through philosophy and empty deceit, according to the tradition of men, according to the basic principles of the world, and not according to Christ. For in Him dwells all the fullness of the Godhead bodily; and you are complete in Him, who is the head of all principality and power." (Colossians 2:8-10)**

Genesis chapter 11 provides the origin of much of the anti-God evil in the world.

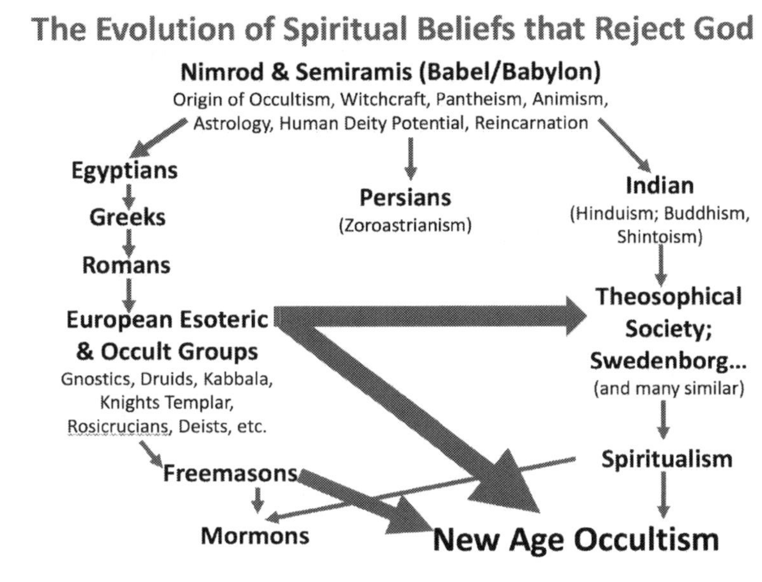

(If you want this chart explained in details, that's in ***"The New Age: The Old Lie in a New Package."*** *- details on back pages.)*

Nimrod and Semiramis were known in:
Egypt as Isis and Osiris
Greece as Orion and Aurora (which means "pregnant with light") also Apollo and Diana or Artemis ("the Mother of gods").
In *Canaan* they were know as Baal and Astarte also as Molech and Ashtaroth, the "Queen of Heaven;"
In *Rome* as Jupiter and Fortuna;
In *India* as Surya (the Sun God) and Isi/Devaki;
The *Scandinavians* called Semiramis Disa;
The *Germans* called her the virgin Hertha;
The *Druids* knew her as Virgo Patitura;
And in *China* as Shing Moo or Ma Tsoopo.
The same basic story went all around the world, with some local variations.

I explained the New Age doesn't want to reject the Christian Church. It seeks to absorb it and change it from within. It has been very successful.

Most interestingly, this poster from the European Union shows their headquarters building as attempting to complete what Nimrod was working on.

EU Building Strasborg - Tower of Babel work in progress. The EU believes they will complete what Nimrod did not.

TRUTH: It's the new hate speech. *"During times of universal deceit telling the truth becomes a revolutionary act,"* so wrote George Orwell.

On the other hand, Adolf Hitler stated *"Make the lie big, make it simple, keep saying it, and eventually they will believe it."*

You have heard parts of THE PLAN, but many people don't seem to have connected all the dots.

It's time we did.

I've heard many conspiracy theories over the years – so have most of you. I always thought some might be possible, but most were just vivid imaginations. I'm left with the suspicion that there has to be more to many of these ones than any of us expected.

Introducing you to the Architect of THE PLAN

Alice Ann Bailey, described as the mother of the New Age, Freemason, Global leader of Theosophical Society, author of "THE PLAN." As such, I refer to her as the Daughter of Perdition, 2 Thessalonians 2:3 explains why.

Alice Ann Bailey was born June 16, 1880 as Alice LaTrobe Bateman, in Manchester, England. She married Foster Bailey on her migration to the USA in 1907 and became known as AAB to her followers, and was an influential writer in what she termed *"Ageless Wisdom."*

This included occult teachings, "mysterious" psychology and healing, astrological and other philosophic and religious themes. Living in the United States she spent most of her life as a writer and teacher, and died December 15, 1949.

Her works, written between 1919 and 1949, describe a wide-ranging system of esoteric or mystic thoughts, covering such topics as how spirituality relates to the solar system, meditation, healing, spiritual psychology, the destiny of nations, and prescriptions for society in general.

She described the majority of her work as having been telepathically dictated to her by a "Master of Wisdom," initially referred to only as "the Tibetan," or by the initials "D.K.," later identified as Djwal Khul." *(Note: Christians call that a demon!)* Her followers refer to her writings as The Alice A. Bailey material, or sometimes, as the AAB material.

She wrote about religious themes, including Christianity, though her writings are fundamentally different from many aspects of Christianity and of other orthodox religions. Her vision of a unified society includes a global "spirit of religion" different from traditional religious forms but included the concept of the Age of Aquarius.

Controversy has arisen around some of Bailey's statements on Nationalism, American Isolationism, Soviet totalitarianism, Fascism, Zionism, Nazism, race relations, Africans, Jews, and the religions of Judaism and Christianity. Alice Bailey was the global leader of the House of Theosophy, an occult organization very influential in the leadership toward the New World Order. She was also a 33 degree Grand Orient Freemason.

(A small explanation here: Grand Lodge Freemasonry (as in Britain, USA, etc.) are all **Pantheistic** - a belief is required in a "Supreme Being" or deity - where any god will do. But Grand Orient Freemasonry (based in France, and mostly found in former Roman Catholic nations) is **Atheistic**. So belief in a deity is not required, and is usually rejected.)

THE PLAN Outlined

#1: Take God and Prayer out of the Education System

#2: Reduce Parental Authority over the Children

#3: Destruction of the Judeo-Christian Family: the Traditional Christian Family Structure for the Western World

#4: If Sex is Free, then Make Abortion Legal and Make it Easy

#5: Make Divorce Easy and Legal, Free People from the Concept of Marriage for Life

#6: Make Homosexuality An Alternative Lifestyle

#7: Debase Art, Make it Run Mad

#8: Use Media to Promote and Change Mind-sets

#9: Create an Interfaith Movement

#10: Get Governments to Make all these (points) Legal, and Get the Church to Endorse These Changes

Freemasonry has been well-positioned to play a vital role in the 4,300 year old dream of Nimrod, a one–world occult kingdom.

Freemasonry currently serves as the bridge between the political organizations of the global elite (Club of Rome, Trilateral Commission, Bilderbergers, CFR, etc.) and the occult groups of the Theosophical network (Theosophical Society, Rosicrucians, Lucis Trust, World Goodwill, etc.)

These groups recognize the position of Freemasonry as an occult religious organization with the ability to bridge the gap between religion and politics.

Charles Finney's revival (mainly on the East Coast of America during the mid-1800s) was preceded by a confrontation of Freemasonry. And the Wesley Brothers' revival was preceded by a confrontation of Freemasonry. The same with Torrey's and Moody's. The revival going on in Argentina today was also preceded by a confrontation of Freemasonry.

Alice and her husband, Foster Bailey, spent years creating a plan of defiance to the core teachings of God! This why she gets my attention!

Let's go through these Ten Steps of THE PLAN for some additional detail.

THE PLAN #1: Take God and Prayer out of the Education System

Alice Bailey wrote: *"Change curriculum to ensure that children are freed from the bondage of Christian culture. Why? Because children go to school to be equipped to face life, they are willing to trust and they are willing to value what is being given to them."*

"If you take God out of education, they will unconsciously form a resolve that God is not necessary to face life. They will focus on those things the school counts them worthy to be passed on and they will look at God as an additional, if one can afford the additional."

NOTE: Most of Academia/Universities have been taken over by anti-God people who are sold-out to this Plan.

But God gave Divine Institutions for the governance of people:
1. Volition - Personal Responsibility - Genesis 2:15-17
2. Marriage - One man and one woman - Genesis 2:22-24
3. Family - Parental authority - Genesis 4:1
4. Human Government - Ruling Authority - Genesis 9:1-17
5. Nationalism - He sets boundaries on nations' borders - Genesis 11:7-9

These Laws are for divine establishment and are principles ordained by God for the orderly function of Individuals, Families and Communities.

THE PLAN #2: Reduce Parental Authority over the Children

Alice Bailey wrote: *"Break the communication between parent and child." Why? So that parents do not pass on their Christian traditions to their children, liberate children from the bondage of their parent traditions.*

Promote excessive child rights; Abolish corporal punishment; (this has been made law). On the other hand the Bible says **'Do not**

withhold correction from a child...' (Proverbs 23: 13-14)

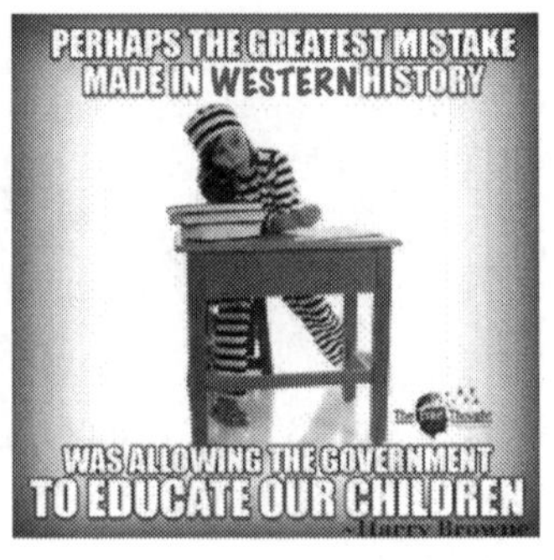

NOTE: Jesus said in the last days, wickedness will increase, there will be rebellion and children will not obey their parents. It is not a trend - it is organized.

Teachers are the agents of implementation – from workshops, teachers tell children 'your parent has no right to force you to pray or read the Bible, you are yourself, have a right of your own, you need to discover yourself.' Self expression, self realization, self fulfilment are all buzz words.

NOTE: In the West when the child is seven years, the teachers begin to say to the child 'you have a right to choose your gender or if you want to follow the faith of your parents or not, parents are not allowed to enforce their faith upon you.' The question is, what type of decision can a seven-year-old make?

This is the saddest photo here: What a tragic mistake to think that secular humanists would educate your children better than you! But God says in His Word, **"Train up a child in the way it should go, and when it is old they won't depart from it." (Proverbs 22:6)**

THE PLAN #3: Destruction of the Judeo-Christian Family: the Traditional Christian Family Structure for the Western World

Alice Bailey wrote: *"It is oppressive that the family is the core of the nation. If you break the family, you break the nation. Liberate the people from the confines of this structure.*

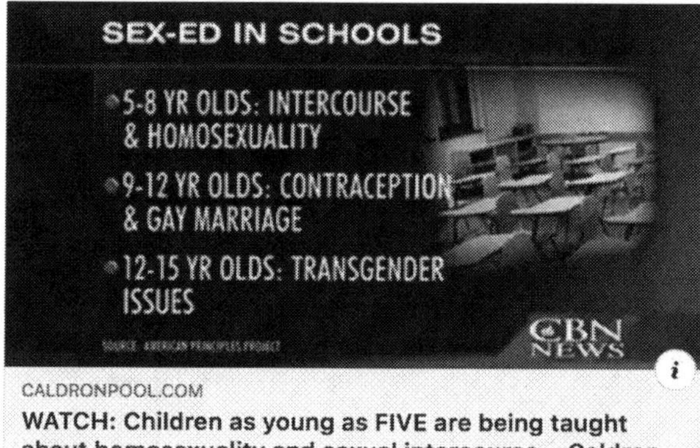

"Promote sexual promiscuity – free young people to the concept of premarital sex, let them have free sex, lift it so high that the joy of enjoying it (sex) is the highest joy in life, fantasize it, that everybody will feel proud to be seen to be sexually active, even those outside of marriage."

NOTE: This is contrary to the word of God which says "**… But fornication and all uncleanness or covetousness, let it not even be named among you, as is fitting for saints… for this you know, that no fornicator, unclean person, nor covetous man, who is an idolater has any inheritance in the kingdom of Christ and God." (Ephesians 5: 3-5)**

"Use advertising industry, media – T.V., magazines, film industry to promote sexual enjoyment as the highest pleasure in humanity." (Propaganda).

Have they succeeded? Have they done it? If you want to see whether they have succeeded or not, go to the advertising industry, it does everything to catch your attention and today almost no advert comes out without a sexual connotation. Even when they advertize ice cream, they must show you a thigh of a woman and a bikini, they must do something to set off a trail of thoughts. They will show you more thighs than ice cream. Why? Because, that is what must be in the minds of the people, according to advertising people.

Announcing ***"I'm Offended"*** is basically telling the world you

can't control your emotions, so everyone else should do it for you. Schools have now become indoctrination centres.

THE PLAN #4: If Sex is Free, then Make Abortion Legal and Make it Easy

Alice Bailey wrote: *"Build clinics for abortion – Health clinics in schools. If people are going to enjoy the joy of sexual relationships, they need to be free of unnecessary fears, in other words they should not be hampered with unwanted pregnancies."*

United Methodist and Episcopalian Church Clergy Lead Prayer Rally to "Bless" Abortion Clinic

In Ohio, United Methodist Church pastor, Reverend Laura Young, says she believes pro-life protesters in front of Planned Parenthood and other...

Abortion as told by Christians is oppressive and denies our rights, we have a right to choose whether we want to have a child or not. If a woman does not want the pregnancy, she should have the freedom to get rid of that pregnancy painless and as easy as possible'.

NOTE: Today abortion is not only accessible but many times it may be forced. It is a strategy to curb population control together with the use of condoms and 'the pill.' (Eugenics)

THE PLAN #5: Make Divorce Easy and Legal, Free People from the Concept of Marriage for Life

Alice Bailey wrote 50 years ago that l*ove has got a mysterious link called the love bond. It is like an ovum that comes out of the ovary, as it travels through your system, it clicks a love favor in you and there's one other person in the world who can respond to that love bond, when you see that person, everything within you clicks, that is your man/woman, if you miss him, you'll never be happy until that love bond cycles past, for many years, so for you to be happy get that person at whatever cost, if it means getting him/her out of*

that marriage, get him/her that is your man/woman. It's a mistake for him/her to be elsewhere. And if you go together for sometime and find that love has died, don't be held in bondage by the Christian values it will never come back, what you need is an easily arranged divorce and allow another love bond to come forth, just like an ovum comes up, and when it comes forth you'll enjoy life again.

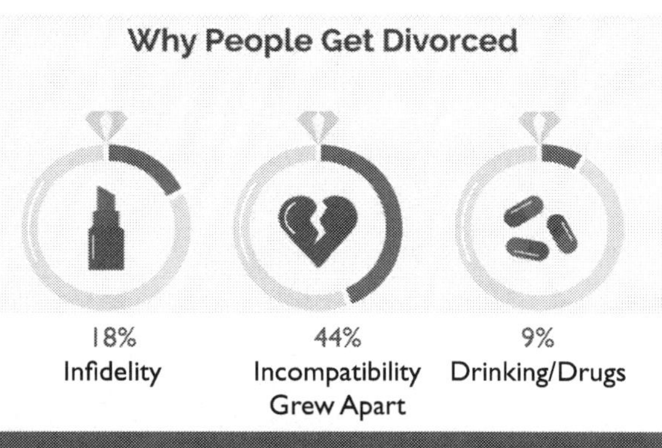

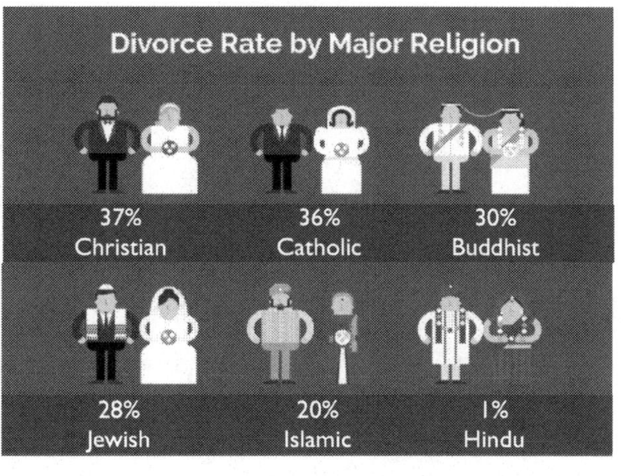

NOTE: On the contrary God's word says in Malachi 2: 16; **"For the Lord God of Israel says that He hates divorce..."** People enter into marriage having signed contracts of how they will share their things after divorce. It is one thing for a marriage to fail but it is another thing for people to enter marriage with an intention to enjoy as long as it was enjoyable and then to walk out of it if it isn't. NOTE: Divorce is not the "unforgiveable sin," blaspheming the Holy Spirit is.

THE PLAN #6: Make Homosexuality An Alternative Lifestyle

Alice Bailey preached that *sexual enjoyment is the highest pleasure in humanity, no one must be denied and no one must be restricted how to enjoy themselves. People should be allowed in which ever way they chose they want, whether it is homosexuality or in incest or bestiality, as long as the two agree.*

NOTE: Many nations around the world are passing laws that legalize homosexual and lesbian 'marriage'. It is now classified as "hate speech" and becoming illegal for ministers of churches and charity organizations to mention homosexuality as an abomination in the eyes of God, or to read Scriptures publicly that talk about homosexuality. Today the church is expected to marry homosexuals/lesbians. Some governments are working on threats to remove tax-exempt status for churches that don't comply. According to the Bible, this is an abomination before the eyes of God (Leviticus 18:22; 20:13).

1. In a sexual species, there are two sexes, MALE & FEMALE.
2. 99.93% of humans have XX or XY sex chromosomes (the rest is a **mutation**)
3. Being one sex but thinking you're the other is a **psychological disorder.**
4. Mandating a widespread enabling of a psychological disorder is **sociopathy**.

Did you know the official flag/logo of the LGBT+ community has only six colors, by missing out indigo. That is the color of royalty, spiritual knowledge and wisdom. God's rainbow has seven colors. By the way, the + that follows LGBT+ refers to sexual relationships with children, we know that as paedophilia, or sex abuse.

THE PLAN #7: Debase Art, Make it Run Mad

Alice Bailey understood that the arts are one of the primary keys to change culture. How? *"Promote new forms of art which will corrupt and defile the imagination of people because art is the language of the spirit, that which is inside, you can bring out in painting, music, drama etc. Look at*

the quality, spirituality and message of the art, music and the films that are coming out."

THE PLAN #8: Use Media to Promote and Change Mindsets

Alice Bailey said *"the greatest channel you need to use to change human attitude is media. Use the press, the radio, T.V, cinema."*

You can tell today how successful they have been in implementing the plan over the last 50 years via media as well as advertising agencies, billboards, magazines. Who controls media?

So much money is pumped into media and advertising and the spreading of violence, pornographic material and other sources. Sex outside of marriage is thrown on your face 80-90 times more than sex in marriage. Promiscuity is being promoted as natural, you can watch gay sex on T.V. in homes where children's minds are being neutralized to sensitivity to these things. You wonder why newspapers, T.V, etc. do not record anything about Christian activities.

According to the Kaiser Family Foundation:

\+ two-thirds of infants and toddlers watch a screen an average of 2 hours a day.

\+ kids under age 6 watch an average of about 2 hours of screen media a day, primarily TV and videos.

\+ kids and teens 8 to 18 years spend nearly 4 hours a day in front of a TV screen and almost 2 additional hours on the computer (outside of schoolwork) and playing video games.

\+ Television Statistics: According to the A.C. Nielsen Co., the average American watches more than 4 hours of TV each day

(or 28 hours/week, or 2 months of nonstop TV-watching per year). In a 65-year life, that person will have spent 9 years glued to the tube or almost 15% of their life.

Three areas of public interest the media has been accomplices in are the climate and environment; gender confusion and Islam.

There has been no recordable increase in global temperatures or sea levels since 2000AD, as shown in this first chart. The average actually continues to show cooling. Claims there would be no ice in the Arctic have proven false, and shipping has been prevented from getting through the North-West Passage due to excessive ice in the past year.

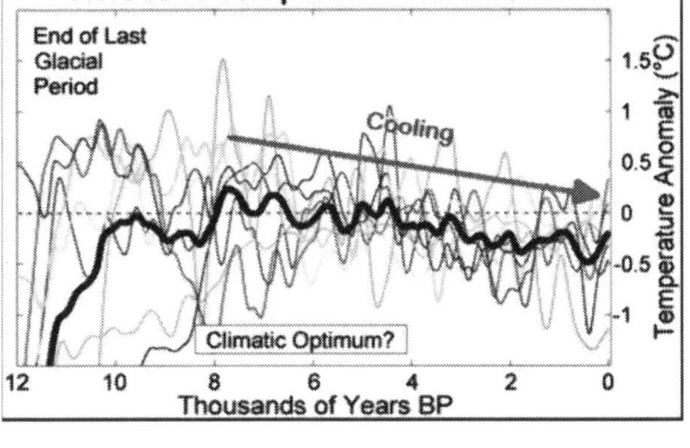

What about the plastic in the oceans? When some 95% of all plastic in the oceans come from just ten rivers (five in China, three more in Asia and the remaining two in Africa - see over page) show that Western nations are not the major culprits in this issue. The nations these rivers flow through need to change their habits and enforce

environmental protections that are clearly required.

DAILYMAIL.CO.UK
95% of plastic in oceans comes from just TEN rivers
Researchers from Helmholtz-Centre for Environmental Research (UFZ) i...

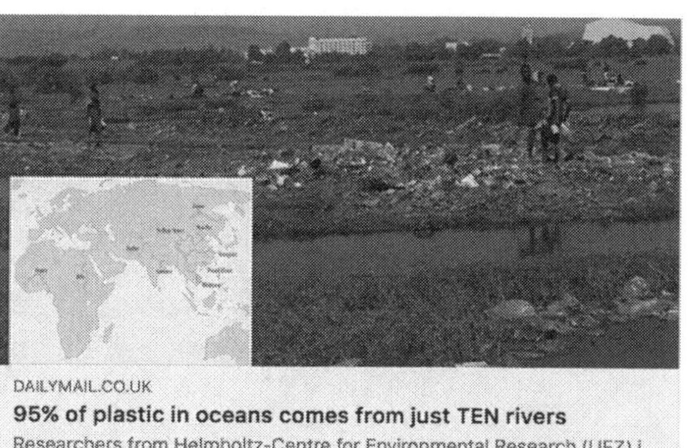

The Mekong, Pearl, Yangtse, Huang, Yunhe, Yellow, Ganges, Indus, Nile, Niger.

The gender confusion issue is covered in Plan # 6.(page 17)

Islam pretends to be a peaceful religion. Fundamentally, Islam is divided into three "Houses." The ***House of Islam*** exists where total control of any nation or society comes from adherence of Islam. Then there is the ***House of War*** - that is everywhere Islam is not in control, and so therefore *Jihad* or war must be waged by followers of Islam until they are victorious. There is a third option, that of the ***House of Truce***. These are the people called "***Dhimmis***" – those who pay tribute because they haven't converted to Islam, (maybe they are Jewish or Christian etc.) yet they have to live in an Islamic society. Under 'Sharia' law non-Muslims must pay tax called "***Jizya***" if they want to live safely under Muslim control, otherwise the state refuses to protect them, even though it protects the Muslim citizens.

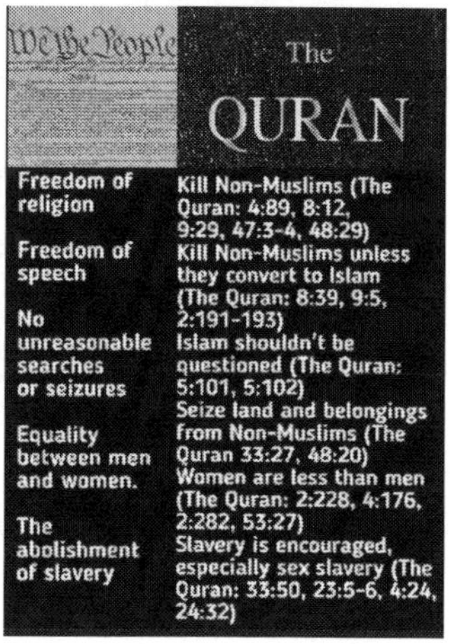
We the People
The
QURAN
Freedom of religion
Kill Non-Muslims (The Quran: 4:89, 8:12, 9:29, 47:3-4, 48:29)
Freedom of speech
Kill Non-Muslims unless they convert to Islam (The Quran: 8:39, 9:5, 2:191-193)
No unreasonable searches or seizures
Islam shouldn't be questioned (The Quran: 5:101, 5:102)
Seize land and belongings from Non-Muslims (The Quran 33:27, 48:20)
Equality between men and women.
Women are less than men (The Quran: 2:228, 4:176, 2:282, 53:27)
The abolishment of slavery
Slavery is encouraged, especially sex slavery (The Quran: 33:50, 23:5-6, 4:24, 24:32)

Recently a minority community of Sikhs was forced to pay Jizya to live safely in a Pakistani region controlled by Taliban. This Jizya is an annual tax, and when it is paid as a "per capita" tax levied all family members of non-Muslim citizens. From the point of view of the Muslim rulers, Jizya was a material proof of the non-Muslims' acceptance of subjection to the Islamic state and its laws. In return, non-Muslim citizens were permitted to practice their faith discretely, to enjoy a measure of communal autonomy, to be entitled to Muslim state's protection from outside aggression. (At least, that's the theory.)

Non-Muslims who pay this head tax or fee are called Dhimmi's. When they pay they are struck in the neck with a chopping motion as a reminder and a threat they will be killed if they break this agreement that has been forced upon them. This explains why there have been so many massacres of non-Muslims in Islamic countries, when Moslems believed these terms had been broken. This has occurred in every century since Mohammed's day, including during the 20th and 21st centuries.

Who is Assimilating with who? We provide refuge, we provide welfare, we allow hundreds of mosques to be built, we allow Islamic ideology into our schools, we allow Sharia law by ignoring it, we are paying a tax on halal food, we allow fully masked people to enter public spaces, we are making exceptions in law. Think about it. We are doing a better job of assimilating into the Moslem way of life than those that should be assimilating into ours.

"Dr. Robert Muller, former Assistant Secretary General of the United Nations, and Chancellor of the United Nations' University For Peace, is the Chairperson of Peace Party 2000." "Decide to open your self to God , the universe, to all your brethren and sisters, to your inner self...to the potential of the human race, to the infinity of your inner self, and you will become the universe...you will become infinity, and you will be at long last your real, divine, stupendous self." Robert Muller, "Decide to Be-Link-up"; p.2

"The underlying philosophy upon which the Robert Muller School is based will be found in the teachings set forth in the books of Alice A. Bailey. The school is now certified as a United Nations Associated School Associated School providing education for international cooperation and peace." Muller, R. "World Core Curriculum." Preface

"Forgetting the things that lie behind, I will strive towards my higher spiritual possibilities. I dedicate myself anew to the service of the Coming One and will do all I can to prepare men's minds and hearts for that event. I have no other life intention." Bailey, A.A. Discipleship in the New Age. Vol. 11. New York: Lucis Trust. p. 226.

NOTE: Alice Bailey wants a unified religion! And which Christ is she preparing for? Not Jesus! The cosmic Christ or Lucifer.

"Evidence of the growth of the human intellect along the needed receptive lines [for the preparation of the New Age] can be seen in the "planning" of various nations and in the efforts of the United Nations to formulate a world plan. From the very start of this unfolding, three occult factors have governed the development of all these plans." Alice Bailey, Discipleship in the New Age (Lucis Press, 1955), Vol.11, p. 35.

Inter-religious Meeting for "Peace of the World" in Graz, Austria, 2002

NOTE: She is not going to tell us exactly what these three occult factors are but she states: *"Within the United Nations is the germ and seed of a great international and meditating, reflective group - a group of thinking and informed men and women in whose hands lies the destiny of humanity. This is largely under the control of many fourth ray disciples, if you could but realize it, and their point of meditative focus is the intuitional or buddhic plane - the plane upon which all hierarchical activity is today to be found."* [Ibid., p. 220.]

NOTE: She is trying to tell us that the inner core of the United Nations is run by people that are under the control of Lucifer.

THE PLAN #9: Create an Interfaith Movement

Alice Bailey wrote: *"Promote other faiths to be at par with Christianity, and break this thing about Christianity as being the only way to heaven, by that Christianity will be pulled down and other faiths promoted."* She said, *"promote the importance of man in determining his own future and destiny"* – HUMANISM. *"Tell man he has the right to choose what he wants to be and he can*

make it happen, he has the right to determine his cause."

The False Claim

Is the True God found in ALL Religions?

Since they contradict each other so much that is unlikely. Here is one example.

* Buddhism, Taoism, Theosophy and New Age Spiritism claim everything is God, including us.

* Hindus and Mormons each have three main gods and we can become gods too.

* Islam, Baha'i and Unitarians each have one distant singular god.

* Judaism, Christadelphians and Jehovah's Witnesses each believe God is singular if not so distant.

* BUT The God revealed through the Bible is infinite, personal, loving, triune, and He wants a relationship with you.

What if: The Bible is not True? There is no Creator God? Jesus isn't the Only Savior? There is no such thing as sin;Therefore no judgement for sin either
What would you stand to lose?

But what if: The Bible is True? A Creator God did make each of us in His own image? Jesus really did die for our sins? Jesus is coming again soon? There is a Judgement Day? What would you stand to lose?

THE PLAN #10: Get Governments to Make all these (points) Legal, and Get the Church to Endorse These Changes

Alice Bailey wrote: *"...that the church must change its doctrine and accommodate the people by accepting these things and put them into its structures and systems."*

Any church that did compromise in the way Alice Bailey suggested would cease to be "Christian" and would become another New Age cult.

A Question for you:

Has ***THE PLAN*** succeeded? Today we wonder why our governments are legislating laws contrary to the Bible and why much of the church is compromising the Word of God. It is a process of implementing this 10 Point Plan - A 70+ year strategy of the NWO to fulfil its ultimate goal to establish a One World Government, a One World Economic system and a One World Religion.(These are the very things I stated in 1992 the New Age wanted. Nothing has changed!)

Today the ***THE PLAN,*** almost in its entirety, has been adopted by the United Nations and much of it is already law in many nations. This deception has crept up by increments, unobserved by most people.(Remember the frog in the kettle.)

NOTE: Today the Western World is not struggling to resist these because the NWO and the New Age Movement focused primarily on the West because that was the Christian world in the 19th & 20th Centuries. The New Age Movement has a school called the Akanni School, which is the school of all the leaders of the Western world.

It is recorded that they say they have succeeded the task in the West but suddenly they realize Christianity has migrated to the rest of the world, so they have now to use every resource in the West to deal with the rest of the world.

I have another question for you:

Have you consented for our children to be educated by a Secular/ Humanist government that:

* Hates God;

* Promotes sexual confusion and promiscuity;
* Turns a blind eye to the hatred spewed from Islam, and actually promotes that;
* Is clearly working to the ***THE PLAN*** to destroy every aspect of Christian faith, Family and observance.

Consent is automatic approval if you have not deliberately withdrawn your consent.

The Plan to Reverse THE PLAN

Some parents are starting to fight back and demand change. This news report came the week prior to my putting this together.

LIFENEWS.COM

700 Parents Show Up to School Board Meeting to Demand School Stop Pushing Sex on Their Kids

In New Zealand, many parents are withdrawing their children from sex-education classes in government schools, because many of them have checked through the curriculum and are not happy with what they read. Most report they prefer Biblical morals to what the State is pushing. The government school system in particular has become the place where ***THE PLAN*** is being implemented, and as Christians, what are we to do?

* The Bible is very clear we are to come out of the Babylonian system and have nothing to do with it, which is a fair description of what we are discussing here.

* A Kingdom-based approach to educating our children would be for several local church fellowships to adopt the Home Schooling materials already available and to take our children out of the State/government school system to prevent further damage to our children, and to repair the damage already done.

* If Christians would come together it would be pretty easy to implement God's Plan and turn this situation around.

* As a smaller nation, New Zealand (as with many nations) had put a lot of value into the United Nations systems. In view of ***THE PLAN*** they have adopted, we all need to re-evaluate the unequal yoking that we have give up our Sovereignty to.

Attitude is important. Let's look at some issues.

UNITY is essential

"Can two walk together, unless they are agreed?"Amos 3:3

A Warning Has Come!

"If a trumpet is blown in a city, will not the people be afraid? If there is calamity in a city, will not the Lord have done it? Surely the Lord God does nothing, unless He reveals His secret to His servants the prophets. A lion has roared! Who will not fear? The Lord God has spoken! Who can but prophesy?"Amos 3:6-8

God's People Need to ACT in UNITY for the sake of our families!

"...the accuser of our brethren, who accused them before our God day and night, has been cast down." Revelation 12:10

"Be sober, be vigilant; because your adversary the devil walks about like a roaring lion, seeking whom he may devour." 1 Peter 5:8

Agreement? OR: Unholy Agreement!

"And they said, "Come, let us build ourselves a city, and a tower whose top is in the heavens; let us make a name for ourselves, lest we be scattered abroad over the face of the whole earth." Genesis 11:4-7

"Perhaps this is the moment for which you were created," (Esther 4:14) said Mordichai to Queen Esther.

I would say this to you: **Don't fear the days ahead, you were made for them!**

So, how should we respond?

First: PRAY!

Protection for Children of Christian families - they are our first concern.
Improvement or removal and replacement of politicians and bureaucrats who are part of ***The Plan.***

Second: Get Organized!

8 to 10 congregations **who love their children** could pool their resources and educate them yourselves. (Some church facilities aren't used 5-6 days each week, that's your schoolhouse!) Some churches are large enough to have their own community school.

There are many organizations for Home-schooling:
Hundreds of thousands already are.

* Back this with prayer and pastoral leadership.
* Find retired or current teachers to supervise them all together.
* Get more parents participating in their children's education. (Not just a few minutes checking homework at night.)

I sensed the Lord say: ***"If this is too much work for you, then why did you have children?"*** It's a parental responsibility to see them grow up in the Lord, their family and community. He also said that ***excuses would come from those who can't discern these issues and don't care enough for their children.***

On the larger scale, clusters of these home-school groups could do sports and other outings, etc. together. Think bigger, arrange regional and inter-regional, even national sports and other competitions.

Third: Plan ahead!

Start working on starting Christian Teachers' colleges, Universities, Polytechnics/Trade Training (all without government control).

Demand of politicians that school fees are 100% deductible (why pay twice for their education?)

This is GOD's Promise - He will restore. Will WE ACT so He can keep His Promise?

It's up to us now!

My father used to say, *"If you don't rock the boat occasionally, you won't know if it's seaworthy."*

My question of the Christian community in this nation is, *"Are you seaworthy?"*

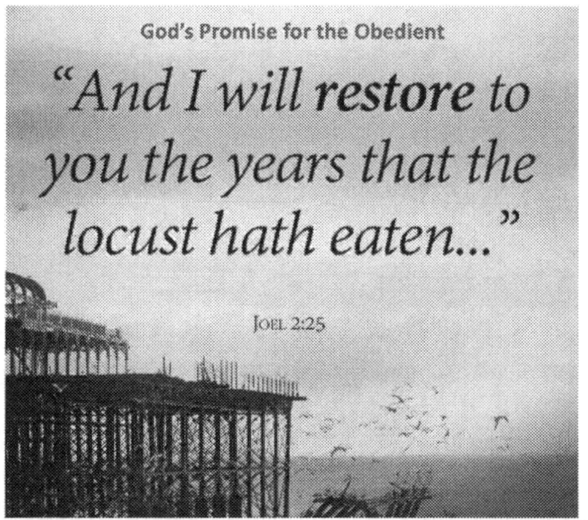

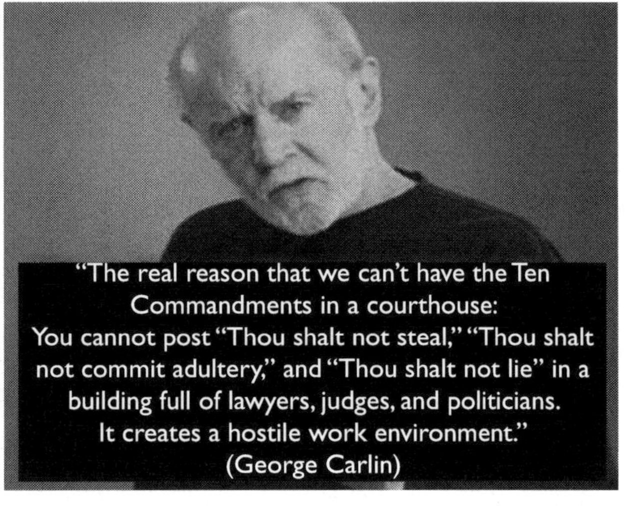

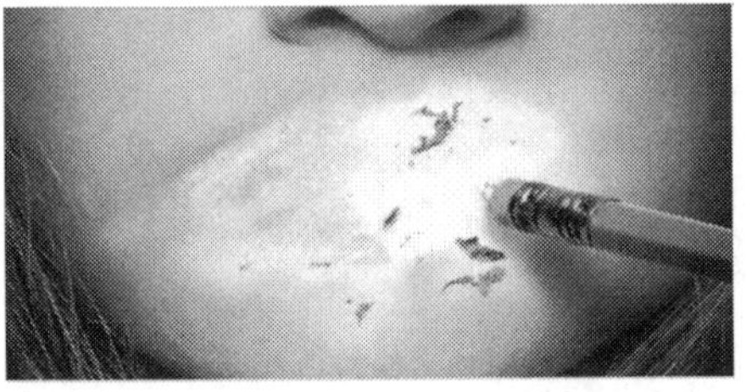

Your opinion is not welcome or valid
if is disagrees with the Elite Authorities

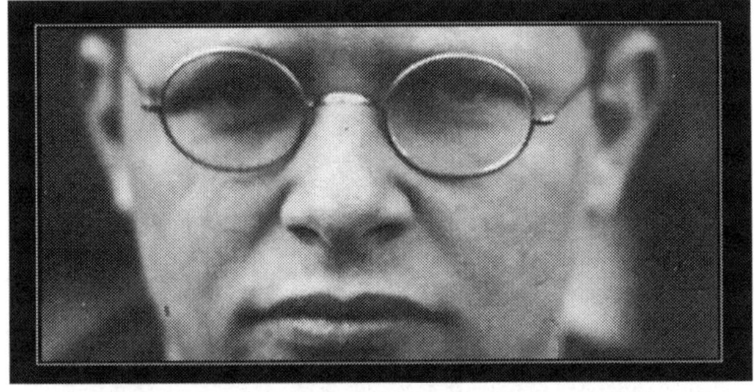

"Silence in the face of evil is itself evil.
God will not hold us guiltless.
Not to speak is to speak!
Not to act is to act!"

Dietrich Bonhoeffer

(murdered by Adolf Hitler for opposing him.)

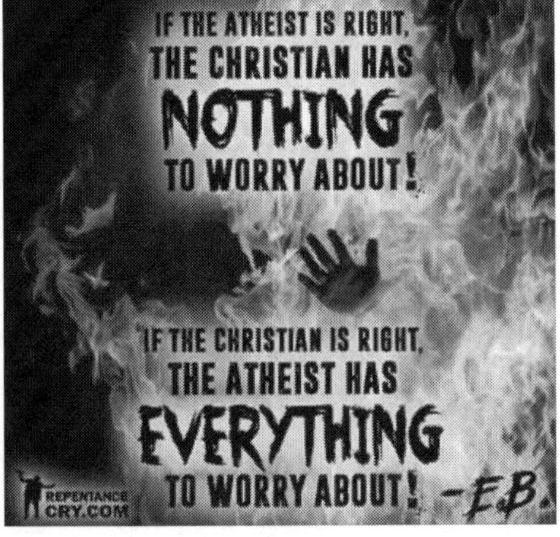

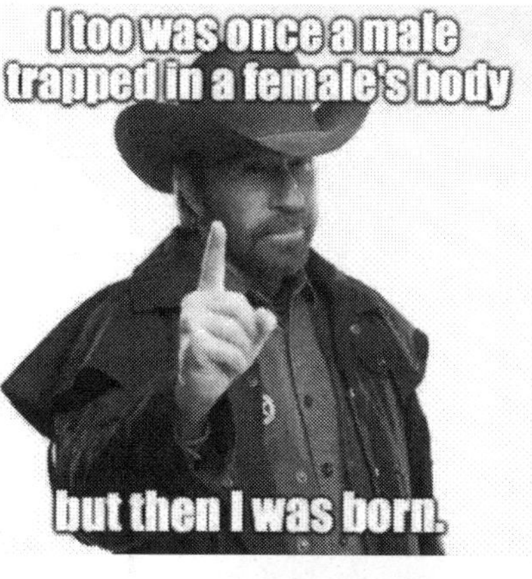

DIAPERS & POLITICIANS
SHOULD BE CHANGED
OFTEN
BOTH FOR THE SAME
REASON

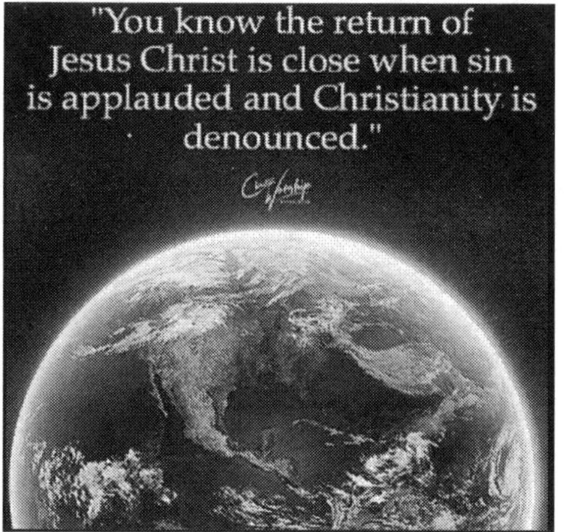

Part Two
THE KING'S PLAN

"Jesus is not the creator of another religion, but the victor over religion; He is not the maker of another law, but the conqueror of law. We call Jesus "the Christ" not because He bought a new religion, but because He is the end of religion. We spread His call because it is the call to every man to receive the New Being... which takes from us labor & burden & gives rest to our souls." (Dr. Paul Tillich, Shaking the Foundation, p 107-108)

"Christianity is not a religion. Christianity is the proclamation of the end of religion, not of a new religion, or even of the best of all religions... If the cross is the sign of anything, it's the sign that God has gone out of the religion business and solved all the world's problems without requiring a single human being to do a single religious thing. What the cross is actually a sign of is the fact that religion can't do a thing about the world's problems – that it never did work and it never will." So stated Dr. Robert Farrar Capon

"Religion demands!
Kingdom Supplies!
Powerful distinction".
said Robert Smith.

I am sometimes asked if I'm religious. My answer is "No!" I know the root meaning of the word results in people being put into bondage. Jesus never called us to do that!

Jesus made four basic calls:

To the unbeliever: **"Come to me, all who labour and are heavy laden, and I will give you rest." Matthew 11:28**

To the believer: **"Come follow Me..." Matthew 4:19**

To the follower: **"...I will make you fishers of men..."Matthew 4:19**

To the disciple: **"Go therefore and make disciples of all nations, baptizing them in the name of the Father and of the Son and of the Holy Spirit!" Matthew 28:19**
To the disciple: **"and what you have heard from me in the presence of many witnesses entrust to faithful men*, who will be able to teach others also." 2 Timothy 2:2** (* anthropoi can refer to both men and women, depending on the context.)

Do you know what a Disciple should be doing? How will we know if you are a Disciple of Jesus? If you were on trial for your life for being a Disciple of Jesus Christ, would there be enough evidence to convict you?

What is a Disciple of Jesus Christ?

There are four main aspects to being a disciple. (Oxford Dictionary)

1. A Believer;
2. A Learner;
3. Someone who is committed; &
4. Someone who fulfills the obligations.

A Believer believes the basics - the foundations of the Christian faith.
They believe God is real and interested in us;
They believe Jesus saves us from our sins;
They believe the Bible is God's Word...

A Believer lives a lifestyle consistent with God's Word.

"Without faith, it is impossible to please God, for he who comes to God must believe that He is, and that He is a rewarder of those who diligently seek Him." (Hebrews 11:6)

A Learner – we might use a term like "pupil" or "apprentice."
A learner in the School of the Messiah.

* An apprentice is someone who learns with the expectation they will do the same with expertise, one day.

* A Learner will be tested to see what they have learned.
* A Learner seeks to apply what they have learned - it must be out-worked, practical.
* A Learner will listen to God's voice. Frequently. (My sheep hear my voice…)
* A Learner is motivated by both love and obedience to the Lord.

"A new commandment I give you; love one another. As I have loved you, so you are to love one another. By this shall all men know you are My disciples, if you love one another." (John 13:34-35)

There are three kinds of Love.

Eros - sexual
Philia - brotherly/family
Agape - the giving type of Love.

"Love suffers long and is kind; love does not envy; love does not parade itself, is not puffed up; does not behave rudely, does not seek its own, is not provoked, thinks no evil; does not rejoice in iniquity, but rejoices in the truth; bears all things, believes all things, hopes all things, endures all things. Love never fails." (1 Corinthians 13:4-8)

Someone who is committed - Not a popular term these days. A true Disciple of Jesus Christ lives a sacrificial life.

"… Whoever does not bear his cross and follow after Me cannot be My disciple." (Luke 14:27)

Being committed means bearing fruit.

"Abide in Me, and I in you," said Jesus. "As the branch cannot bear fruit of itself, unless it abide in the vine, neither can you unless you abide in Me. I am the vine, you are the branches. He who abides in Me and I in him, bears much fruit; for without Me you can do nothing." (John 15:4-5)

The term "convert" only occurs 9 times in the New Testament. Compare that with "disciple" occurs 269 times in the Four Gospels and the Book of Acts alone. God is still looking for disciples for His Son – not mere converts.

Being committed also means
* Being sent out under authority
* Accountable
* Teachable

One Who fulfills the Obligations

A Disciple of Jesus Christ is one who shares their faith with others.

"And He (Jesus) said to them, "Go into all the world and preach the Gospel to every creature." (Mark 16:15)

"Preach" here means making it relevant to the audience.

Discipline comes from the same root word as Disciple. It implies instruction and correction when we get it wrong. It means training that "improves, molds, strengthens and perfects character."

"When you pray…" (Matthew 6:7) Not ***"If you pray…"***

Discipling others.

Who are you discipling?
We all need a 'Paul' and a 'Timothy'

Train them to read the Bible – the Three Questions to ask, and Answer
* What does it Say?
* What does it Mean?
* How should this be applied in my life today?

Train them to share their faith with others.

Train them to heal the Sick (see Mark 16:17-18)

"… As you go, preach the message: 'The Kingdom of Heaven is near', Heal the sick, raise the dead, cleanse those with leprosy, drive out demons. Freely you have received, freely give." (Matthew 10:7-8)

"All authority has been given to Me in heaven and on earth. Go therefore and make disciples of all nations, baptizing

them in the name of the Father and of the Son and of the Holy Spirit, teaching them to observe all the things I have commanded you; and lo, I am with you always, even to the end of the age." (Matthew 28:18-20)

From this we learn Jesus has all authority.

We are to make disciples - not converts;
Baptize disciples into the Godhead; *(but not into a church denomination.)*
Teach them to do (not just to watch);
We are not alone.

"But you shall receive power when the Holy Spirit has come upon you; and you shall be witnesses to Me in Jerusalem, and in all Judea and Samaria, and to the end of the earth." (Acts 1:8)

The proof is recorded in Acts 4:31:

- They were assembled together, praying
- The place was shaken
- All were filled with the Holy Spirit
- All spoke the Word of God with boldness
- All went out and demonstrated ministry without fear
-

The fastest-growing parts of the Christian church are demonstrating Signs and Wonders in healing.

Why did Jesus regularly use miracles in front of crowds of people?

So they would believe in Him!

Summary of the miracles of Jesus:
* There were sixteen straight healings
* There were eight expulsions of demonic spirits.
* There were five provisions of fish, food or money.
* There were three raised from the dead.

There was one each of
* turning water into wine;
* disappearing;
* calming a storm;
* walking on water; and
* cursing a fig tree.

Some Christians remain on milk for decades. Sometime they may do a Bible study on some good subject such as healing. They tell people they have had some "real meat".

No they haven't! They just ate the menu. The Bible is the menu; the meat is to do the will of the Father - to perform the miracles and healing and other graces of God.

If you are hungry for meat, you will be doing the Word, not just hearing or reading it, according to John 4:34.

God's Plan for Health & Healing

Biblical Healing is an essential ingredient in evangelism, as well as through every church fellowship's mercy ministries, and must be outworked by every believer in the Lord Jesus Christ.

To equip those in their church ministry teams how to minister healing at the front of their church during or following their normal church service, at a time when healing should be offered;

To equip those in leadership of home/house/cell groups (where much ministry should be occurring) so there is safe and dignified

healing available, amongst other ministry matters such as teaching the word, etc.;

To equip those Disciples of Jesus Christ who would choose to be obedient to His command, to offer healing to those they come across on a daily basis. This can include over the fence with neighbors; at work, shopping at the mall, walking down the street, etc.

Five IF's of Sustainable Healing

If …you diligently heed the voice of the LORD your God and do what is right in His sight, give ear to His commandments and keep all His statutes, I will put none of the diseases on you which I have brought on the Egyptians. For I am the LORD who heals you." Exodus 15:26

It's NOT unconditional

If…My people who are called by My name will humble themselves, and pray and seek My face, and turn from their wicked ways, then I will hear from heaven, and will forgive their sin and heal their land." 2 Chronicles 7:14

Humility and submission to God.

If …I regard iniquity in my heart, The Lord will not hear." Psalm 66:18

God goes deaf if we stay in sin.

"Then Jesus said to those Jews who believed Him, If you abide in My word, you are My disciples indeed. And you shall know the truth, and the truth shall make you free." John 8:31-32

We need to apply truth.

"…by which also you are saved, If you hold fast that word which I preached to you - unless you believed in vain." 1 Corinthians 15:2

Obedience and consistency.

Religious people always get upset when God uses the people they thought were unqualified!

Jesus said to the followers, "Go everywhere in the world. Tell the Good News to everyone. Anyone who believes and is baptized will be saved. But he who does not believe will be judged guilty. And those who believe will be able to do these things as proof: They will use my name to force demons out of people. They will speak in languages they never learned. They will pick up snakes without being hurt. And they will drink poison without being hurt. They will touch the sick, and the sick will be healed."

After the Lord Jesus said these things to the followers, he was carried up into heaven. There, Jesus sat at the right side of God. The followers went everywhere in the world and told the Good News to people. And the Lord helped them. The Lord proved that the Good News they told was true by giving them power to work miracles. (Mark 16:15-20 *International Children's Bible*) – so even the simple get it!

The Emphasis of Three Kinds of Churches:
Traditional - social justice issues
Evangelical - Bible-based lecture halls
Holy Spirit-led - gifts (healing, prophecy…)

Real followers of Jesus Christ should be doing all three.

Virginia Marshall dissected these three for me:
"Traditional & Evangelical churches have taught us God forgives sins, and when we die, we go to heaven to be with the Lord forever. 100% true.

Charismatic & Pentecostal churches have taught us God not only saves but He also heals our diseases, sends Holy Spirit to live in us and empower us to operate in spiritual gifts and fruit. Also 100% true.

And we have now moved into a much deeper level of understanding about the goodness of God. This is an age of Sonship and governmental authority. He is in us and we are in Him. The shift in our thinking is from being a servant, to being a Son or Daughter of God."

As Virginia explain, *"We are sons and daughters who serve, rather than a servant who happens to be children of God. For example, the Prodigal Son story isn't about the son. It's about the goodness of the Father. The son wanted to come back as a servant, but the father wouldn't let him. He insisted on taking him back as a son. And we are often like the older brother who doesn't realize we have full access to Dad's entire Kingdom as soon as we are born again and became sons and daughters of God."*

I said there are three kinds of churches. But, there is another kind.

The Fourth Kind: Learning to be the Ecclesia

Book of Acts Ecclesia
For three hundred years the Christian Church was home-centered:
* Just believers coming together in their homes to worship (Acts 13:2)
* Praise God (Acts 2:47),
* Pray (Acts 12:5),
* Read the Scriptures (1 Timothy 4:13),
* Encourage one another (Hebrews 10:24-25),
* Sing (Ephesians 5:19, Colossians 3:16),
* Listen to the apostles' teaching (Acts 2:42),
* Have a meal together (Acts 2:46),
* Have the Lord's Supper (1 Corinthians 11:22)
* Heal the sick, cast out demons… (Mark 16:16-20)

We have all been taught that the term "Ecclesia" means *"the called-out ones"*. Called out for a special purpose; to fulfil God's Kingdom purposes .

Dr. Derek Prince states in his last book, ***"Rediscovering God's Church"*** *"In the contemporary secular Greek of the New*

Testament times, the word ecclesia had a very specific meaning. It meant a "governmental assembly".

"Some therefore cried one thing and some another, for the assembly [ecclesia] was confused, and most of them did not know why they had come together." Acts 19:32

"But if you have any other inquiry to make, it shall be determined in the lawful assembly. [ecclesia]" Acts 19:39

"And when he had said these things, he dismissed the assembly [ecclesia]" Acts 19:41

"Thus, the root meaning of the word we habitually translate as church actually means a "legal or governmental assembly." (Dr. Derek Prince, "Rediscovering God's Church" p 26)

Tyndale's Bible, the first English translation to work directly from Hebrew and Greek texts, properly translated "ecclesia". He refused to use the word "church". For this, he was strangled and burned, by the church leaders. His dying prayer was for God to open the King of England's eyes for the need of Scripture in the language of the people.

Later the decisive shift towards official mistranslation came with Article 3 of King James's 15 Edicts which governed the translation of the King James Version.

Article 3: "The old Ecclesiastical Words to be kept, viz. the Word "Church" not to be translated "congregation", "assembly" etc.

Every modern translation picks up this bias.

Who or what constitutes an Ecclesia?

"He said to them, "But who do you say that I am?" And Simon Peter answered and said, "You are the Christ/Messiah, the Son of the living God." Jesus answered and said to him, "Blessed are you, Simon Bar-Jonah, for flesh and blood has not revealed this to you, but My Father who is in heaven." Matthew 16:15-17

"And I also say to you that you are Peter, and on this rock I will build My ecclesia, and the gates of Hades shall not prevail against it. "And I will give you the keys of the kingdom of heaven, and whatever you bind on earth will be bound in heaven, and whatever you loose on earth will be loosed in heaven." Matthew 16:18-19

The true Ecclesia can only include those who have received the revelation of the divine, eternal nature of Jesus Christ as the Son of God, the Messiah, and the soon-returning King of Kings!

"...whatever you bind on earth will be bound in heaven, and whatever you loose on earth will be loosed in heaven."

That means what you prohibit or what you permit.

"Your kingdom come, Your will be done on earth as it is in heaven." Matthew 6:10

Do you think God wants people involved in prostitution, burglary, drug-pushing, idolatry, etc.

These things are happening around us in also every community.

By neglect and ignorance, we have permitted them.

What would change in your community if the Ecclesia gathered in your home prohibited those types of things in your community?

"The cold makes us shiver, and great heat causes us pain, but a lukewarm bath is comfort itself. Such a temperature suits human nature. The world is always at peace with a Lukewarm church, and such a church is always pleased with itself", so stated noted preacher, Charles Spurgeon

The Healer didn't come to heal because you prayed to be healed. The Healer came so that the people watching the healed would believe in The Healer!

The God gets all the glory!!!!!

"And these signs shall only follow the 12 apostles and then die out with them" - Things the REAL Bible doesn't say...

"You have made the commandment of God of no effect by your tradition." (Matthew 15:6b)

"No one can make us as uncomfortable as the comforter ...He's about to make the Church very uncomfortable ...because He loves us and those who He loves He disciplines," Kathie Walters stated.

Separation is coming between church followers and Jesus followers; Between those who go to church, and those who go to Jesus Christ!

**Apostles BUILD,
Prophets REVEAL,
Pastors NURTURE,
Teachers EXPLAIN,
Evangelists GATHER.
We need them ALL**

We are moving past the church age as we enter into Kingdom Governmental Authority, as One in Messiah and under Him alone, by the Holy Spirit. Interestingly, over the past three or four decades, there's been a move towards the Biblical leadership format of the Five-Fold ministry as God instructed in Ephesians 4:11 and following, (which also confirms their job description). The CEO-style of most churches was never Biblical.

"Jesus drank the cup of wrath without mercy so that we may drink the cup of mercy without wrath."

The World has all but forgotten about God, and I have a feeling He's about to remind us who He is.

The GREAT Awakening will be preceded by the RUDE Awakening I can't help but wonder how many of today's preachers would

have told Shadrach, Meshach, and Abednego they should just take a knee...???

Far too much of what has been taught to Christians lacks Biblical foundations. When presented with actual truth, they whine, hide behind their error or heresy, or accuse people of fake views.

The Bereans were applauded because they checked things out to see if they were true. That's called being "Teachable!"

So, in summary, we now have the opportunity to obey the King's command:

"Go therefore and make disciples of all nations, baptizing them in the name of the Father and of the Son and of the Holy Spirit!" Matthew 28:19

"...and what you have heard from me in the presence of many witnesses entrust to faithful men, who will be able to teach others also." 2 Timothy 2:2

My father told me that while he didn't expect to see the Return of Jesus, he expected us boys to. He's long been promoted to the Lord's presence, and we are all still here. While there are a few Scriptural prophecies remaining to be fulfilled, the vast majority have been.

In the meantime, He told us to **"Occupy until I come,"** (Luke 19:13). That means getting on with our responsibilities of advancing the Kingdom of God.

You are not too bad to come in.
You are not too good to stay out.

Try Jesus.
If you don't like Him,
the devil will always
take you back.

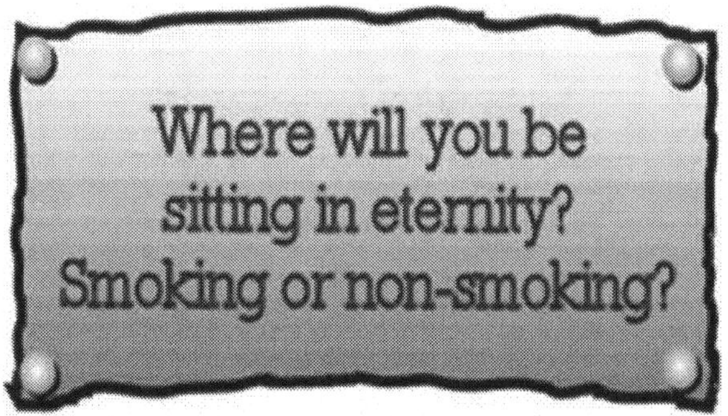
Where will you be
sitting in eternity?
Smoking or non-smoking?

Appendix One
THIS GOSPEL OF THE KINGDOM

Before we look at this topic, let's ask ourselves six questions that should aid us in our study.

1. How many of us love Jesus?

2. How many of us are grateful for what Jesus did for us at Calvary?

3. How many of us believe the Bible is God's Word for us?

4. How many of us know about "The Great Commission" that Jesus spoke of in Matthew 28?

5. How many of us believe we each have a responsibility to participate in this command of Jesus?

6. How many of us believe Jesus Christ could return in the lifetime of many readers?

I hope you are able to agree with all of these!

Jesus proclaimed, "This gospel of the Kingdom shall be preached in the whole world for a witness to all nations, and then the end shall come" (Matthew 24:14)

We need to understand that the Biblical gospel consists of two parts - "the good news about the kingdom of God" and "the name of Jesus".

"But when they believed Philip as he preached the things concerning the kingdom of God and the name of Jesus Christ, both men and women were baptized." (Acts 8:12).

Is there some way to summarize this gospel of the kingdom?

Is it possible to reduce the essence of it down to something we can know and share with others?

My first assumption is that this may be an impossible task without being too wordy. Most people will give up listening if we just get "preachy".

Acts indicates that Jesus spent his last 40 days on earth explaining the kingdom of God to his disciples.

"...to whom He also presented Himself alive after His sufferings by many infallible proofs, being seen by them during forty days and speaking of the things pertaining to the kingdom of God". Acts 1:3

If there is that much material to know and understand, what possible chance do we have of knowing it well enough to share it with others?

We know that the disciples DID go out with this message, but they likely did not try to get potential converts to commit to a daily 6-week training course in order to "be saved." The Apostle Paul, in particular, did spend extended time teaching about the gospel of the kingdom

"And he went into the synagogue and spoke boldly for three months, reasoning and persuading concerning the things of the kingdom of God". Acts 19:8

However, there apparently must have been a "shorter version" of the kingdom gospel that the Early Church shared. Otherwise it seems unlikely that the message would have ever gone out.

While I think that it may be risky to try and reduce the gospel of the kingdom down to a simple formula, I believe that we each need to have a basic "kingdom gospel outline" to work from in order to share this essential message with others. Before I suggest to you a possible outline, let me point out some serious mistakes that have been made in the past by those trying to do something similar.

The Four Spiritual Laws

Maybe you have heard of "The Four Spiritual Laws." They are the

result of the efforts of some to come up with a simple formula for easily sharing the gospel. As such, these "Laws" are:

1. God LOVES you and offers a wonderful PLAN for your life.

2. Man is SINFUL and SEPARATED from God. Therefore, he cannot know and experience God's love and plan for his life.

3. Jesus Christ is God's ONLY provision for man's sin. Through Him you can know and experience God's love and plan for your life.

4. We must individually RECEIVE Jesus Christ as Savior and Lord; then we can know and experience God's love and plan for our lives.

Sounds like a good, simple system for sharing the gospel, right? The only problem is that these ***"Spiritual Laws"*** don't include the good news about the kingdom. They are all about *"the name of Jesus"* but not about his role as King of the Kingdom.

The Roman Road

Another popular tool for sharing the gospel is often called "The Roman Road". It consists of these points:

1. Romans 3:23 **"For all have sinned and fall short of the glory of God."**

2. Romans 6:23a **"...The wages of sin is death..."**

3. Romans 6:23b **"...But the gift of God is eternal life through Jesus Christ our Lord."**

4. Romans 5:8, **"God demonstrates His own love for us, in that while we were yet sinners Christ died for us!"**

5. Romans 10:13 **"Whoever will call on the name of the Lord will be saved!"**

6. Romans 10:9,10 **"...If you confess with your mouth Jesus**

as Lord, and believe in your heart that God raised Jesus from the dead, you shall be saved; for with the heart man believes, resulting in righteousness, and with the mouth he confesses, resulting in salvation."

Again, this is a fairly simple gospel presentation to remember and share, but again it doesn't include the ***"gospel of the kingdom."***

So, let me share with you some basics that might work for a ***"Gospel of the Kingdom"*** presentation. Perhaps we can work together to refine, complete and revise this outline.

1. The ultimate plan of God is bring the earth back to perfection, as it was in the beginning;

2. God has appointed His Son, Jesus, to be the King of this perfect future age;

3. Jesus came into the world the first time to announce the coming of the hidden Kingdom ("the mysteries of the kingdom") and to prepare for the future visible Kingdom. (Isaiah 9:7);

4. Jesus came to pay the price for all people's sin by his death on the cross, burial, and resurrection from the dead;

5. Those who accept Jesus' sacrifice by faith are granted forgiveness of sin, inner renewal through Holy Spirit, and hope of immortality in the coming Kingdom (Colossians 1:13);

6. Believers are brought into the present hidden Kingdom (Revelation 1:6; 5:10) and are placed in training to co-rule the earth with Jesus in the future Kingdom. (Daniel 7:18) This training consists of a Godly lifestyle (1 Thessalonians 2:10-12) and good stewardship of time and talents.

Let me give you with a simple illustration that helps me see a bit more clearly the difference between "the gospel" and "the gospel of the kingdom."

If we talk about Jesus as a person we can focus on His strengths – His teaching authority, His compassion, even His sacrificial death. We basically come away with the picture of "a nice guy" not unlike other great teachers throughout the ages. But when we put Him in the perspective as King of the coming Kingdom we begin to see a dynamic Jesus – not a "nice guy" trapped in history, but a King who is alive and building His Kingdom today, and preparing to return to rule the world.

I believe this is the Jesus of the Bible, and this is the Jesus we need to know and share.

Dr. Jack Hayford writes, *"The most essential idea for each believer to grasp is found in the words of Jesus,* ***"This gospel of the Kingdom shall be preached in the whole world for a witness to all nations, and then the end shall come" (Matthew 24:14).*** *After coming to know salvation through Jesus Christ, God's Son, it is essential for us to gain a practical perspective on all that is included in this one verse in the Bible. This perspective will help us recognize and grow into a fully developing, Biblical lifestyle that distinguishes between traditionalized Christianity, and dynamic Christ-honoring life, growth and ministry. The "Gospel of the Kingdom" points not only to a message, but to a mind-set – to a recognition that Jesus Christ wants to fill every one of His disciples with His life, love and power, to make them a ministering member of His body (Ephesians 1:15-23)."* (Hayford's Bible Handbook, p. 622)

Dr. Hayford concludes, *"The truth of "The Kingdom of God" studied in its fullness opens the door to a life*
1 growing in the truth of God's Word;
2 Revealing the love of God's Son;
3 and serving in the power of God's Spirit".

Dr. Hayford made a comparison between "traditionalised Christianity" and "dynamic Christ-honoring life, growth and ministry". The latter is to do with relationship; our relationship with God. The former is to do with rituals, rules and denominational control. I can't think of a more simple way of describing this vital and fundamental difference.

If a believer today contrasts the traditional Christian message to the simple message of Jesus recorded in the gospels, we must conclude that the two messages are very different. It becomes apparent that the message taught and preached by Jesus and the apostles after Him has been set aside and "another gospel" has been embraced and emphasised in the Church. This "other gospel" is universally received today as the orthodox Christian massage.

The Kingdom of God

The message of Jesus was the "Kingdom of God". He declared that He had been sent to preach this message, **"But He said to them, 'I must preach the kingdom of God to the other cities also, for I was sent for this purpose'" (Luke 4:43).**

Some implications concerning the establishing of God's kingdom include:

A. Every form of human government will be abolished. This will include international, national, state and local. Every constitution written will be voided because the government will **"rest on His shoulders" (Isaiah 9:6).**

B. Human self-determination will end. "Every knee will bow, of those who are in heaven, and on earth, and under the earth, and that every tongue should confess that Jesus Christ is Lord, to the glory of God the Father" (Philippians 2:10-11).

C. The false dreams and illusions of man will be extinguished completely. God is the God of reality (Jeremiah 10:10).

D. Israel will be the only national entity that survives in the kingdom. As God's elect nation, it will be exalted high above all the nations for praise, fame and glory (Deuteronomy 26:19).

E. Jesus taught continually by parables to convey the basic message of the Kingdom. Prior to the time of Jesus, the Kingdom of God was envisioned as God's reign in Israel in the manner that occurred during the First Temple era. God was manifested during this era through His indwelling glory in the Temple and through His anointed prophets, priests and kings. Jesus introduced a new

perspective of the Kingdom of God and began to lay the foundation for the establishment of this Kingdom during His earthly ministry. It would take millennia for its complete realisation.

F. God would rule directly through the indwelling Holy Spirit in the hearts of believers. This was the fulfilment of the prophecy spoken by Ezekiel that God would: **"Moreover, I will give you a new heart and put a new spirit within you; and I will remove the heart of stone from your flesh and give you a heart of flesh. And I will put My Spirit within you and cause you to walk in My statues, and you will be careful to observe My ordinances." (Ezekiel 36:26-27).**

G. Jesus also introduced the concept of the "Living Temple". His body was the temple during His earthly ministry. After His ascension the church would function in this capacity. Ultimately this "Living Temple" would be established in Jerusalem just like the First Temple had been. As a "living stone" of this temple the individual believer was positioned or seated in the presence of the Living God.

Many aspects of the Kingdom of God were introduce by Jesus as He taught His disciples in parables. These aspects of the Kingdom of God began being fulfilled through the early church; they have continued to be fulfilled for almost 2000 years. The vision outlined by these parables will not be fully realised until Jesus returns and reigns in Jerusalem directly in the midst of Israel.

Another Gospel

Now today, when we consider the basic message of the Church, we hear something different from Jesus' message of the Kingdom of God. The Church message focuses on the reconciliation of individuals to God. Paul outlined this message in his second letter to the Corinthians

"Now all things are of God, who has reconciled us to Himself through Jesus Christ, and has given us the ministry of reconciliation, that is, that God was in Christ reconciling the world to Himself, not imputing their trespasses to them, and

has committed to us the word of reconciliation. Now then, we are ambassadors for Christ, as though God were pleading through us: we implore you on Christ's behalf, be reconciled to God". 2 Corinthians 5:18-20

Indeed, this is a valid message for the Church to share in the midst of the nations. Nevertheless, as is obvious from our discussion of Jesus' message, the message of reconciliation in no way encompasses the Kingdom message taught by Jesus. The Church has basically spiritualized the Kingdom message and focused on the message or vision of reconciliation, which has been fairly faithfully set forth in the nations. Every denominational group has emphasized different aspects of this message, yet it is fundamental to all branches of the Church.

Evidently, the Church determined to de-emphasize Jesus' message and substituted the message of reconciliation in its place. There are a number of reasons for this.

Firstly, the message of reconciliation is a "good, positive" message causing little reproach to the one who proclaims it. The Kingdom message, on the other hand, is like a sword causing a polarization in those who hear ***"Do not think that I came to bring peace on earth. I did not come to bring peace, but a sword", Matthew 10:34***. The one proclaiming the Kingdom message must bear reproach.

A second reason why the Church de-emphasized the Kingdom message is that God's Kingdom, as preached by Jesus, is intimately linked with Israel and Jerusalem. The Church succumbed to the pressure to adopt a universal identity while rejecting identity with Israel. Therefore, Jesus' message became awkward for them. The message of reconciliation, on the other hand, was easily adapted to the universal identity.

A final reason why the message of reconciliation was emphasized so strongly by the Church is that it was in the process of forming a new world religion, Christianity, distinct from that which preceded it. Like all religions it mapped out a way to come to God. The message of reconciliation served this purpose very well. The

Kingdom message was unprofitable in the formation of this new religion.

There is probably any number of other factors that influenced this transition, but these three should be sufficient to outline for us why the message of reconciliation was emphasized at the expense of the Kingdom message. Today, this whole sequence is simplified in the minds of Christians by the rationalization that the message of Paul is the highest form of revelation available to us. They proclaim that Jesus preached His message to Israel, who they claim rejected it; therefore, God anointed Paul to bring forth this new universal message. Hence, the Church vision is logically built on Paul's message or letters rather than on the message of Jesus.

Today, as God has re-established the people of Israel in the Land of Israel, the Kingdom message is being preached again with a fresh anointing. With end-time events rapidly being fulfilled, we are beginning to focus on the King and His message of the Kingdom. Indeed, this in itself is a sign of the end. Jesus proclaimed, **"This gospel of the Kingdom shall be preached in the whole world for a witness to all nations, and then the end shall come" (Matthew 24:14).**

Jesus was not speaking of the "gospel of reconciliation", which has been set forth by the Church for almost two millennia. He was speaking of the message of the Kingdom of God. The message of reconciliation could be preached to every living soul and we would not necessarily be nearer the goal of seeing the kingdom established. It is the message of the Kingdom that must be proclaimed.

The Mystery of the Miraculous

There are many aspects of the miraculous to our faith. For example, Jesus was born of a virgin. That's rather miraculous. Healing was a major part of Jesus' ministry. In fact healing is covered in every book in the Bible, so this is a significant activity in God's Kingdom. Rather poorly recognized in many church congregations today, healing still is part of our brief as followers of Jesus Christ.

Scripture also proved Jesus' ability to forgive sin:
"But that you may know that the Son of Man has authority on earth to forgive sins...." He said to the paralyzed man, "I tell you, get up, take your mat and go home." (Luke 5:24)

Salvation requires belief in the heart:
"That if you confess with your mouth, "Jesus is Lord," and believe in your heart that God raised him from the dead, you will be saved". (Romans 10:9)

Many believe because of the miracle:
"But if I do it, even though you do not believe me, believe the miracles, that you may know and understand that the Father is in me, and I in the Father." (John 10:38)

Deliverance from evil spirits was also part of Jesus' ministry. Deliverance was a power statement declaring the end of the dominion of darkness and the advancement of God's Kingdom in a given person's life. *(For further teaching on this, I suggest my book, "Dealing with Demons".)*

I believe that's enough to understand that the miraculous is fundamental to the faith in God and His Kingdom.

What is the gospel of the kingdom?

"Kingdom" is made up of two words – "King" and "Domain". We see the kingdom revealed in the ministry of Jesus

It is the place of God's government. Jesus is subject to the leading and rule of His Father. He does nothing without the Father telling Him.

"So Jesus said, "When you have lifted up the Son of Man, then you will know that I am the one I claim to be and that I do nothing on my own but speak just what the Father has taught me". (John 8:28)

Sins are forgiven; not just to get saved and go to heaven.

People are healed; spirit, soul and body.

Jesus will return to rule this world as King

“Then the seventh angel sounded: And there were loud voices in heaven, saying, “The kingdoms of this world have become the kingdoms of our Lord and of His Christ, and He shall reign forever and ever!” (Revelation 11:15)

The kingdom has a mysterious aspect that isn’t always obvious to the casual observer.

“He told them, “The secret of the kingdom of God has been given to you. But to those on the outside everything is said in parables”” (Mark 4:11)

We are told the kingdom is within us. Once, having been asked by the Pharisees when the kingdom of God would come, Jesus replied,

“The kingdom of God does not come with your careful observation, nor will people say, ‘Here it is,’ or ‘There it is,’ because the kingdom of God is within you.” (Luke 17:20-21)

Christ in us the hope of Glory. This, too, is a mystery to those not yet in His Kingdom, including a lot of folks going to church regularly.

“To them God has chosen to make known among the Gentiles the glorious riches of this mystery, which is Christ in you, the hope of glory”. (Colossians 1:27)

When we have the kingdom within, we have the leading of God from within. In fact, this should become the government of God **within us**.

It is an internal, not an external rule, by the Holy Spirit.

“This is the covenant I will make with the house of Israel after that time,” declares the Lord. “I will put my law in their minds and write it on their hearts. I will be their God, and they will be my people. No longer will a man teach his neighbor, or a man his brother, saying, ‘Know the Lord,’ because they will all know me, from the least of them to the greatest,” declares the

Lord. "For I will forgive their wickedness and will remember their sins no more." (Jeremiah 31:33-34)

"Write it on their hearts..." We need to consider this further.

"But the Helper, the Holy Spirit, whom the Father will send in My name, He will teach you all things, and bring to your remembrance all things that I said to you. (John 14:26)

Please allow me to give you a vital revelation: Inner guidance comes from an intimate relationship with the Lord . The Holy Spirit will teach, lead, guide and discipline each of us as required.

"Because those who are led by the Spirit of God are sons of God. (Romans 8:14)

Stop and think for a moment: are you led by your own wisdom or instincts, (your will) or are you led by the Holy Spirit? If not by the Holy Spirit, is this Scripture suggesting those who aren't are not God's children? That is a sobering thought we need to give urgent consideration to. Jesus gave us the template of this relationship of obedience:

Jesus gave them this answer: **"I tell you the truth, the Son can do nothing by himself; he can do only what he sees his Father doing, because whatever the Father does the Son also does. For the Father loves the Son and shows him all he does. Yes, to your amazement he will show him even greater things than these". (John 5:19-20)**

"For I did not speak of my own accord, but the Father who sent me commanded me what to say and how to say it. I know that his command leads to eternal life. So whatever I say is just what the Father has told me to say". (John 12:49-50)

Let's consider this powerful revelation: We are to do the same things as Jesus, and if we do, we will see similar results to those recorded about Him;

"I tell you the truth, anyone who has faith in me will do what

I have been doing. He will do even greater things than these, because I am going to the Father". (John 14:12)

I have seen God open blind eyes, and deaf ears. I have taken photographs of two people God raised from the dead, and have met over a dozen different people in New Zealand whom God used to raise others from the dead. I have been in the homes of three of these people. They seek no glory for themselves, they are just glad God chose to use them in these ways. *(For further teaching on this issue, check out my book, "Where Have All the Miracles Gone?")* The massive increase in the Christian faith globally is through the miraculous in healing, deliverance etc. and prophetic gifting released.

Jesus prayed that we may be one as He and the Father are one:

"I have given them the glory that you gave me, that they may be one as we are one: (John 17:22)

Eternal Life is knowing the Father and Jesus:

"Now this is eternal life: that they may know you, the only true God, and Jesus Christ, whom you have sent". (John 17:3)

It's not a place, but a relationship. Therefore eternal life is about relationship. God comes and lives inside you so you can do things for Him. It's not to get saved, but because you are.

Jesus told unbelievers that God lived in him and the miracles prove it:

"But if I do it, even though you do not believe me, believe the miracles, that you may know and understand that the Father is in me, and I in the Father." (John 10:38)

Paul taught relationship with God – the full gospel of the kingdom and the inner guidance of the Holy Spirit

"By the power of signs and miracles, through the power of the Spirit. So from Jerusalem all the way around to Illyricum,

I have fully proclaimed the gospel of Christ". (Romans 15:19)

Paul states that he left nothing out of his message, and look at his fruit:

"But what things were gain to me, these I have counted loss for Christ. But indeed I also count all things loss for the excellence of the knowledge of Christ Jesus my Lord, for whom I have suffered the loss of all things, and count them as rubbish, that I may gain Christ and be found in Him, not having my own righteousness, which is from the law, but that which is through faith in Christ, the righteousness which is from God by faith". (Philippians 3:7-9)

Baptism is an essential ingredient to move forward in our faith in Christ. It has power and purpose in God's Kingdom. That is why I've included it as the third appendix in this book. The essential issue is that Biblical baptism is a command of the Lord Jesus Christ by those old enough to ask for it and who do so to fulfil righteousness, as Jesus Himself stated.

"...Permit it to be so for now, for thus it is fitting for us to fulfil all righteousness". Matthew 3:15

(When John was trying to prevent Jesus from being baptized, claiming the Jesus should baptize John.)

Biblical baptism involves a dying to self and an identification with Jesus Christ and His Kingdom.

We need to die to independence or you won't hear God's voice clearly. There is often an Ishmael before an Isaac - the self puffed up before the Holy Spirit deflates us to His purpose. It isn't about your ministry, but His ministry through you.

Personal Inner Guidance

So, boiled down, the gospel of the kingdom is revealed by inner guidance from the Holy Spirit. Another way of writing about the kingdom would be to replace it with the term, **"personal inner guidance."**

A word of caution: we need to be careful that God's Holy Spirit is the source of this guidance. We don't want a familiar spirit guiding us, as practiced by Spiritualists, Mormons and other occultists.

Let's look at some Scriptures, by adding that term so we can better understand what God is trying to get through to us.

"And this gospel of the kingdom (inner guidance) will be preached in the whole world as a testimony to all nations, and then the end will come". (Matthew 24:14)

"But seek first his kingdom (personal inner guidance) and his righteousness, and all these things will be given to you as well". (Matthew 6:33)

"I tell you, among those born of women there is no one greater than John; yet the one who is least in the kingdom of God (personal inner guidance) is greater than he". (Luke 7:28)

"I tell you the truth, anyone who will not receive the kingdom of God (personal inner guidance) like a little child will never enter it". (Luke 18:17)

"So was fulfilled what was spoken through the prophet: "I will open my mouth in parables, I will utter things hidden since the creation of the world." Then he left the crowd and went into the house. His disciples came to him and said, "Explain to us the parable of the weeds in the field." He answered, ...Then the righteous will shine like the sun in the kingdom of their Father. He who has ears, let him hear. "The kingdom of heaven (personal inner guidance) is like treasure hidden in a field. When a man found it, he hid it again, and then in his joy went and sold all he had and bought that field. "Again, the kingdom of heaven is like a merchant looking for fine pearls. When he found one of great value, he went away and sold everything he had and bought it". (Matthew 13:35-46)

Again Paul shows us the value he places on knowing Christ in an ongoing relationship, and the righteousness that flows from that:

"But whatever was to my profit I now consider loss for the sake of Christ. What is more, I consider everything a loss

compared to the surpassing greatness of knowing Christ Jesus my Lord, for whose sake I have lost all things. I consider them rubbish, that I may gain Christ and be found in him, not having a righteousness of my own that comes from the law, but that which is through faith in Christ—the righteousness that comes from God and is by faith". Philippians 3:7-9

The end-time church will seek intimacy with God. This is already evident. Reports are growing from around the world of Christians gathering to pray, to worship God in fresh and non-religious ways.

Exercise

Consider this Scripture:

"I no longer call you servants, because a servant does not know his master's business. Instead, I have called you friends, for everything that I learned from my Father I have made known to you". John 15:15

Why do you think Jesus said this?

Ask the Holy Spirit *"What are you saying to me personally Lord?"*

Then read this and ask the same questions:

"Behold, I stand at the door and knock. If anyone hears My voice and opens the door, I will come in to him and dine with him, and he with Me". (Revelations 3:20)

Why do you think Jesus said this?

Ask the Holy Spirit *"What are you saying to me personally Lord?"*

We need to Know God

To recognize is *"to identify, to realize and discover the nature of, to admit or acknowledge the existence or validity or character or claims of,'* according to the Oxford Dictionary.

I find that a very useful definition. To "hear" means to perceive with the ear, to listen to, and to be informed.

Jeremiah 9 speaks about the one thing we should boast about is that we understand and know God.

"Thus says the LORD: "Let not the wise man glory in his wisdom, let not the mighty man glory in his might, nor let the rich man glory in his riches; but let him who glories glory in this, that he understands and knows Me, that I am the LORD, exercising lovingkindness, judgment, and righteousness in the earth. For in these I delight," says the LORD." (Jeremiah 9:23-24)

John describes about knowing Jesus.

"And this is eternal life, that they may know You, the only true God, and Jesus Christ whom You have sent". (John 17:3)

John also speaks about loving God and obeying His teaching.

"Jesus answered and said to him, "If anyone loves Me, he will keep My word; and My Father will love him, and We will come to him and make Our home with him". (John 14:23)

There are many other Scriptures that speak about God's desire that we would know Him, that we would have relationship with Him, and every relationship includes two way communication.

Man cannot know God unless God first chooses to know us. God always initiates the relationship with us, so He clearly wants one with each of us.

14 "I am the good shepherd; and I know My sheep, and am known by My own."
27 "My sheep hear My voice, and I know them, and they follow Me". (John 10:14 & 27)

Recognizing God's voice means first we hear it, then we get the

revelation about what is said, and by whom; and then we have the choice to obey and act on that guidance as appropriate, or not.

A guide is one who shows the way, and guidance is being led safely.

There are a number of thoughts relating to guidance. It can imply an intimate knowledge of the way, including the difficulties and dangers, and also going ahead to show the way (this especially applies with those with leadership responsibilities) so that others may follow.

Guidance implies an ability to keep on the course that God has laid out, and sometimes that can be difficult. If we come across difficulties we might avoid them or overcome them. This carries with it a concept of obedience; to obey is to carry out a command, to do what one is instructed to do.

The Plans of God

All through Scripture and history God has had a plan for the lives of His people. He had a plan for Adam and Eve, He had a plan for Abraham, to take him out of idolatry, He had a plan for the salvation of the people of Israel to come out of Egypt, He had a plan for His people whose disobedience placed them in bondage to the Babylonians. God had a plan for Jesus,

"Then He took the twelve aside and said to them, "Behold, we are going up to Jerusalem, and all things that are written by the prophets concerning the Son of Man will be accomplished". (Luke 18:31)

This shows that Jesus had a specific plan for His disciples. He still has plans for each of us too.

Jesus' main purpose on Earth was to do the Father's will.

"Jesus said to them, "My food is to do the will of Him who sent Me, and to finish His work" (John 4:34).

"Then I said, 'Behold, I have come - in the volume of the book

it is written of Me - to do Your will, Oh God.' Previously saying, "Sacrifice and offering, burnt offerings, and offerings for sin You did not desire, nor had pleasure in them" (which are offered according to the law), then He said, "Behold, I have come to do Your will, Oh God." He takes away the first that He may establish the second". (Hebrews 10:7-9)

There are many other examples we could use showing Jesus' willingness to obey His Father, just as we should.

All through the Book of Acts we see the plan God had for the disciples. In Paul's case it was to take the message of the Kingdom through Jesus Christ to the non-Jews - the Gentile nations. What is God's plan for your life? Are you putting yourself in the place where they can be fulfilled? That's a sobering thought we need to consider carefully.

Let us look at some Scriptures on guidance.

"I will instruct you and teach you in the way you should go; I will guide you with My eye". (Psalm 32:8)

"The LORD will guide you continually, and satisfy your soul in drought, and strengthen your bones; you shall be like a watered garden, and like a spring of water, whose waters do not fail". (Isaiah 58:11)

"Show me Your ways, Oh LORD; Teach me Your paths. Lead me in Your truth and teach me, For You are the God of my salvation; On You I wait all the day". (Psalm 25:4-5)

"In all your ways acknowledge Him, and He shall direct your paths". (Proverbs 3:6)

"He restores my soul; He leads me in the paths of righteousness For His name's sake". (Psalm 23:3

"However, when He, the Spirit of truth, has come, He will guide you into all truth; for He will not speak on His own authority, but whatever He hears He will speak; and He will tell you things to come". (John 16:13)

What does this guidance look like?

In the Old Testament, guidance by the Holy Spirit came through physical sense, such as dreams, visions, burning bushes, through audible voices, and through visitations by angels. Sometimes the Holy Spirit came on people for a season, to achieve a purpose. This was particularly true of prophets, much of whose statements were recorded in the Old Testament.

Because of the New Covenant, we are adopted into God's family so we are given the Holy Spirit to live as a seal of our sonship, regardless of gender:

"In Him you also trusted, after you heard the word of truth, the gospel of your salvation; in whom also, having believed, you were sealed with the Holy Spirit of promise." (Ephesians 1:13)

So the Holy Spirit is the main source of communication to obedient followers of God today.

"For as many as are led by the Spirit of God, these are sons of God. For you did not receive the spirit of bondage again to fear, but you received the Spirit of adoption by whom we cry out, "Abba, Father." The Spirit Himself bears witness with our spirit that we are children of God". (Romans 8:14-16)

"But the Helper, the Holy Spirit, whom the Father will send in My name, He will teach you all things, and bring to your remembrance all things that I said to you". (John 14:26)

There are many similar Scriptures.

Getting it right!

I do need to raise one important issue here. Some immature people will take these Scriptures to mean they can do what they want, as long as they claim the are obeying God. Many of us have met people like this, and frequently they fit in two main categories. Either they are rebellious to legitimate Biblical authority, or they need to start taking their medication again. I have discussed this with various pastors and leaders over the years, and one of the hardest things to

deal with are people who are convinced that God has told them to do something specific, which may not be correct. However, no-one can argue with them; their opinions hold them firmly.

If you are facing a major decision, and sense God is speaking to you about it, God doesn't mind honest questioning to ensure you have heard correctly before you race off and possibly make a mistake. Why not seek prayerful involvement with two or three mature and obedient followers of Jesus, to confirm God's will. When there is unity of the Spirit together, the answer will be obvious.

On the other hand, there are too many pastors and leaders who like the power to control people. Such controllers don't like teaching that includes that you can hear from God directly, you don't need a medium such as a priest to determine what God means in Scripture, for example. These controllers are empowered by the Nicolaitan spirit that Jesus had such harsh words about in Revelation 2:15. (To *address this and related issues isn't my brief here, so I recommend "The Three Doctrines of Damnation" by Dr. Dale Sides)*

Summary For Guidance

I noticed in the **Old Testament** that God spoke in a number of ways. He spoke face to face to Adam, to Cain, Noah, Abraham, and to Moses. He spoke audibly out of a cloud, out of a burning bush, out of a donkey to Balaam, to Elijah in a whisper, to Samuel during the night. God spoke by dreams to Jacob, Abimilech, and Joseph and to many of the prophets. He also spoke by visions to prophets, to Uzziah the King, to Ezekiel, Samuel, Daniel. Over 100 times in the Old Testament God spoke by angels to Hagar, to Abraham, to Moses, Lot, Zachariah and others. On a few occasions God spoke by writing on stone tablets, or walls. Sometimes He spoke by signs such as Gideon's fleece, and also by miracles, such as when He parted the Red Sea, healed Namaan the leper, and through Moses during the time under Pharaoh.

In the **New Testament**, God used similar methods to communicate; He spoke by dreams to Mary and Joseph, for the outpouring of the Holy Spirit by vision, Peter on the roof, and Paul about the man from

Macedonia. God spoke out loud at the Mount of Transfiguration, at Jesus' baptism, and to Paul on the road to Damascus. There was a two-way communication with John the Baptist's father, Zachariah, in the Temple and Paul on the road to Damascus. Sometimes God used angels, to Zachariah, to Mary and Philip. Other times God spoke through the Holy Spirit, such as to Peter when he was sent to the home of Cornelius, the sending out of Saul and Barnabas as missionaries and to be kept from preaching to Asia also.

Jesus also spoke and we heard from God through Him, and we also have the Bible, which Jesus quoted from frequently, as did the New Testament writers. We now have the whole Bible, so God has a way of speaking to and with us, if we feed on His Word. Just reading is helpful, but when God provides a Rhema word, breathed by the Holy Spirit, the written word leaps off the page at us with revelation and power. The Gifts of the Holy Spirit include ways for God to speak to us, through 1 Corinthians 12 and 14, including prophecy, Words of Knowledge and Wisdom, etc.

You can study the Bible all your life, and get an understanding of what you think it says, but without the Holy Spirit you won't get the true understanding. In some church denominations (and even in cults), there is a great deal of emphasis on study, learning and knowledge, but Scriptures says ***"Knowledge puff's up"*** (1 Corinthians 8:1) but what we need to revelation. That provides us with understanding, which is spiritually discerned.

For most of the time between the early church in the Book of Acts, and today, religious education has been about knowledge, especially for those who end up in pastoral roles in local congregations. Theology is an intellectual exercise that can never discover the hidden mysteries of the Kingdom of God and these Jesus imparted to His disciples. Study isn't the issue; revelation is the issue.

The supernatural power and the heavenly wisdom of God are not obtained through intellectual study, because the Bible is a spiritual book, and only comes alive when the student has the Holy Spirit, and when your heart attitude is to hear and obey what God wants. The intellectual knowledge of the Bible can only produce opinion,

and there are too many opinions. That is part of the reason we have so many denominations. Men have divided over their interpretations of Scripture. But God wants individuals and a Church that is in relationship with Him. He wants us hearing Him by the Holy Spirit. Unity of the Holy Spirit should be our goal.

"But Peter and John answered and said to them, "Whether it is right in the sight of God to listen to you more than to God, you judge. For we cannot but speak the things which we have seen and heard". (Acts 4:19-20)

Power to Act

Paul the Apostle shows that there are two main issues about hearing from God. One is spiritual maturity, and the other is loving God.

"However, we speak wisdom among those who are mature, yet not the wisdom of this age, nor of the rulers of this age, who are coming to nothing. But we speak the wisdom of God in a mystery, the hidden wisdom which God ordained before the ages for our glory, which none of the rulers of this age knew; for had they known, they would not have crucified the Lord of glory. But as it is written: "Eye has not seen, nor ear heard, nor have entered into the heart of man the things which God has prepared for those who love Him." But God has revealed them to us through His Spirit. For the Spirit searches all things, yes, the deep things of God". (1 Corinthians 2:6-10)

"Jesus answered him, "The first of all the commandments is: 'Hear, Oh Israel, the Lord our God, the Lord is one. 'And you shall love the Lord your God with all your heart, with all your soul, with all your mind, and with all your strength.' This is the first commandment. "And the second, like it, is this: 'You shall love your neighbor as yourself.' There is no other commandment greater than these". (Mark 12:29)

Let me close with two vital Scriptures:

"My sheep hear My voice, and I know them, and they follow Me". (John 10:27)

"This gospel of the Kingdom shall be preached in the whole world for a witness to all nations, and then the end shall come". (Matthew 24:14)

Even so, come Lord Jesus!

Appendix Two

CHRISTIAN BAPTISMS

Introduction

The subject of Christian baptism is sometimes controversial, because many people have differing thoughts about this practice. Some doubt that it is important, while others debate how it should be done.

According to the Bible there are actually three forms of baptism. The first and main form understood by people involves water. There are also clear references to Baptism of the Holy Spirit, and with fire at Pentecost. (Matthew 3:11; Luke 3:16; Acts 2,3). John pointed to Jesus as the one who baptizes with the Holy Spirit (John 1:33)

Our purpose here is to examine what the Bible actually does say about these topics, and to see if we can sort out the myths from the Biblical commands and practices. It is very important for all who call themselves Christian to be certain of what God requires from us in this issue of baptism, as in all things.

What does "Baptism" mean?

The Greek word for baptism is *baptizo,* from which we get *'baptisma',* which is the process of immersion, submersion and then emergence, according to Vines Expository Dictionary. The root word is *'bapto'*, which means to dip. This is the word that is used in the Bible to speak of John's baptism, of Christian baptism, and also the baptism of suffering that Christ underwent at Calvary, (see Luke 12:50).

From this we also get another term, *'baptismos'*, which is used to speak of the ceremonial washing of articles. This act of baptism uses the same word the Greeks used to signify the dyeing of a garment by full immersion in a vat of color dye.

When a garment is dyed to change its color this new color goes right through the fabric. The original color is overcome and replaced.

One Biblical illustration of this is the reference in Isaiah 1:18, in which the Lord says,

"Though your sins are like scarlet, they shall be as white as snow."

This means that our sins are forgiven and removed.

This leads us to a very important point. Baptism, on its own, does not mean that we are changed or forgiven. Baptism states the fact of an event that has already happened. Baptism must be an outward sign of an inward reality. The inward reality is that we have recognized that our sin separates us from God, that we have surrendered to Jesus and invited Him to be Lord and Savior of our life. The Bible calls this "being born again," (John 3:3).

So why be baptized?

A. Baptism is a command. **"He who believes and is baptized will be saved..." (Mark 16:16)**. Belief MUST precede baptism.

B. We are commanded to follow the example of Jesus. **"For to this you were called, because Christ also suffered for us, leaving us an example, that you should follow His steps," (1 Peter 2:21).**

C. Baptism identifies us with Christ, His death, burial and resurrection. **"...All of us who were baptized into Christ Jesus were baptized into His death. We were therefore buried with Him through baptism into death, in order that, just as Christ was raised from the dead through the glory of the Father, we too may live a new life," (Romans 6:3-4 NIV).**

Who should be Baptized?

Certain standards were required prior to baptism in the New Testament. Let us look at some of these.

John **"went into all the region around the Jordan, preaching a baptism of repentance for the remission of sins," (Luke 3:3).**

Jesus said, "Go therefore and make disciples of all the nations,

baptizing them in the name of the Father and of the Son and of the Holy Spirit," (Matthew 28:19).

Jesus also said "Go into all the world and preach the gospel to every creature. He who believes and is baptized will be saved..." (Mark 16:15-16).

Jesus commanded this to all believers in Him; not just clergy.

Peter said to them "Repent, and let every one of you be baptized in the name of Jesus Christ for the remission of sins; and you shall receive the gift of the Holy Spirit"... "Then those who gladly received his word were baptized..." (Acts 2:38,41).

"...And many of the Corinthians, hearing, believed and were baptized," (Acts 18:8).

There are many other similar passages, but there is a distinct pattern emerging. First, people believed because they were taught the Word of God, then they repented, and only then were they baptized.

John the Baptist challenged people to **"Bear fruit worthy of repentance..."** prior to baptism, (Luke 3:8). It hardly needs to be said that a person cannot repent of sin if they haven't heard God's Word first. So repentance and surrender to Jesus Christ is necessary prior to baptism in the New Testament.

In Acts 10:45-48, Peter's immediate response was that these people needed to be baptized. That followed their obvious conversion. In Acts 22:12-16, a religious man was confronted by Jesus on the road to Damascus and blinded. Ananias came to Saul/Paul three days later and physically healed his sight. This allowed time for reflection and repentance. Ananias then prophesied over him, and only then told Saul/Paul to be baptized.

Baptism was an immediate result of conversion, usually done the same day. In fact, there is no such thing as an un-baptized Christian in the New Testament.

How is Baptism to be done?

Water is used to perform baptism. How much? John baptized Jesus and many others in a river. The Disciples used this same method while Jesus was there, and this continued through the Book of Acts by the Apostles. Some references don't say how this was done, while others mention a pool was used. There are many references to ***"coming up out of the water,"*** such as Matthew 3:16 and Acts 8:39.

Believer's baptism by full immersion was the only Christian practice recorded for the first twelve or so centuries after Christ. In Old Testament times when a Gentile (non-Jew) converted to the Jewish faith they undertook a ritual immersion - *mitkveh.*

What about Infant Baptism?

Some Christian denominations practice "infant" or baby baptism, usually by 'sprinkling' with a few drops of water. This is sometimes called 'Christening'. In the Orthodox (Greek and Russian etc.) Churches, infants are baptized by immersion up to their neck.

During the Dark Ages (when the church had adopted paganism and Anti-Semitism as a life-style, and thereby devalued itself by becoming a political organization instead of being life-changing through the Holy Spirit), a particular problem arose. People practicing witchcraft got the weird notion that if they sacrificed a person who hadn't been "baptized", that person would go to hell rather than heaven. Children were at obvious risk. (This concept has no Biblical basis to it, of course.) The Bishop of Rome at the time simply declared that baptizing infants would overcome this dilemma, which it largely did.

In a council of the Church held at Ravenna in 1311, Pope Clement V declared that, *"It is a matter of indifference whether immersion or sprinkling is used."*

One of the ablest Roman Catholic theologian, Rev. S.J. Hunter, SJ, in his "Outlines of Dogmatic Theology", remarks, "*It is impossible for infant baptism to be discussed directly between a Catholic and a Baptist. They have no common ground. The Baptist urges that the Scriptures everywhere teach faith as a prerequisite to baptism. The*

Catholic defends his practice as to infants by the authority of the (Roman Catholic) Church, which the Baptist refuses to recognize," (Vol.3, page 222).

Rev. Hunter goes on to say, *"The great bulk of Protestant sects employ infant baptism. Yet there is no trace in Scripture of Christian baptism being administered to anyone who was not capable of asking for it.* ***The practice of infant baptism, therefore, cannot be defended on Scriptural grounds,"*** (Vol.1, page 148). (Emphasis added)

"The change from the ordinary rite – from immersion to sprinkling – was made by the authority of the (Roman Catholic) Church, which is sufficient". (page 216)

The Roman Catholic Church has consistently claimed that the official teaching of their Church is equal in authority with the Bible. The Reformation, started by Martin Luther and others, was the result of those who chose to believe the authority of the Bible above all other authority. This is what Rev. Hunter is commenting on above. Roman Catholics practice infant sprinkling because their church says they can, and they make no pretence to obey Scripture.

Other Christian denominations who practice infant sprinkling cannot claim the authority of the Bible for their practice of sprinkling infants, as Rev. Hunter points out. There is no apparent reason for this practise other than that Pope Clement said they could do it that way.

The 'baptism' of babies gives a false sense of spiritual security to its recipients, who are often strangely resistant to later appeals, as if inoculated against the gospel. It was Martin Luther who termed infant baptism as ***"Unbeliever's Baptism"***.

Fundamentally, "Christening" or "infant baptism" is the dedication of a child to God (or to that church denomination) with water. As such, it fails the Biblical standard of baptism that requires a person to be old enough to believe in Jesus Christ and who personally accepts and affirms what Jesus did on Calvary's cross for them.

Confirmation by an authority such as a bishop in later life is a poor substitute for the Biblical model. Recipients of 'Christening' or infant sprinkling need to be informed that they have not yet received Christian Baptism. When they come to faith in Jesus Christ they still need to obey the Biblical command to be baptized.

Did Baptism Replace Circumcision?

There are those who claim that infant baptism took the place of the Jewish rite of circumcision. But only male infants were circumcised eight days after birth. Circumcision was the seal of a covenant between God and the nation of Israel. God had chosen them for a special work. The written law, under significant penalty, bound them to circumcise every male child. There was no female equivalent. Regardless of gender, all children were dedicated to the Lord. This also happened with Jesus when He was a baby. Christians through the ages who practice Believer's Baptism usually dedicate their children as well. (Luke 2:22-23)

"In Him (Jesus) you were also circumcised, by the putting off of the sinful nature, not with a circumcision done by the hands of men but with the circumcision done by Christ, having been buried with Him in baptism, and raised with Him through your faith in the power of God, who raised Him from the dead," (Colossians 2:11-12 NIV).

This is plain enough. An eight-day old boy doesn't know he has a sinful nature and needs to repent and put his faith in God. And why should girls miss out on salvation? They shouldn't! Baptism is not a substitute for the Old Covenant practice of circumcision. Jesus and the Apostles never even hinted that it might be.

The New Testament refers to five cases of ***"believing households"*** being baptized. (John 4:53, Acts 10:2, 16:32, 18:8, 1 Corinthians 16:15). Children are not mentioned in any of them, but every reference said that every member of the household believed God. It would be safest to assume, with no contrary evidence available, that all family members were old enough to repent of their own sins prior to baptism by immersion. Any claims to the contrary are unfounded speculation not supported by the Biblical text.

Baptism and the New Covenant

Baptism, on the other hand, is a sign of the New Covenant established between God and the believer. When a person accepts Jesus Christ as Savior and Lord, he or she enters into a new relationship with God. In obedience to the command and example of Jesus, the believer submits to baptism as an outward sign of this change. Jesus and the Apostles emphasize the fact that this change is a personal and voluntary one.

Baptism by Proxy

As I am completing this writing, there is news that Mormon Church leaders have apologized for their proxy baptisms of many Jewish people killed during the Holocaust of World War Two. Mormons believe that people can be converted to their version of eternity after they have died. This false doctrine has no Biblical basis at all, and is rejected and denied by Hebrews 9:27, which says, **"It is appointed for men to die once, and then to face judgement".** This false practise of proxy baptism comes from a faulty understanding of 1st Corinthians 15:25, where Paul the Apostle is explaining about resurrection. Paul nowhere supports this practise of proxy baptism. Neither do any other writers of Scripture.

Baptize in what name?

Jesus instructed the Disciples to baptize in **"the name of the Father and the Son and the Holy Spirit,"** when He gave them the Great Commission, (Matthew 28:19-20). This makes sense when we consider that we are called to proclaim the Kingdom of God, so it should be done in the name of God as revealed through His tri-unity as Father, Son and Holy Spirit.

There are references in the Book of Acts where Peter and Paul told people to be baptized into the Name of Jesus. This was to distinguish Christian baptism from the baptism of John, (see Acts 2:38, 8:16, & 19:3-5). These do not cancel or negate the clear teaching of Jesus given in Matthew 28. There are some religious groups who baptize people in the name of Jesus only. These people wrongly reject the deity of both the Father and the Holy Spirit. This is most common amongst groups that could best be described as cultic, due to their erroneous understanding of clear Bible teaching on these and related topics.

Baptism is not the same as church membership, and should not be confused with it. Baptism will neither save nor condemn a person. Salvation is through Jesus Christ, not through baptism. **"Salvation is found in no one else, for there is no other name under heaven given to men by which we must be saved," (Acts 4:12 NIV).**

Who Can Baptize others?

Prior to John the Baptist, self-baptism was the usual method in Hebrew society and religious life. There seems to be no evidence of one person being baptized by another prior to John. However, after John, the standard procedure involving baptism was that the new convert was baptized by the person who had just explained the Gospel message and led them to faith in Christ. In cases where a large number were involved, a team might be used to assist with mass baptisms. The only requirement was for two believers to act as witnesses to the event. This seems to be the minimum required for a person to receive New Testament Baptism.

However, in many traditional church denominations ordained clergy, such as a pastor, minister or priest, usually performs baptism. (Note: a significant proportion of these denominations do not practice Believers or New Testament/Biblical baptism, but a form of sprinkling. This clearly shows where denominational tradition, rather than the Bible, has replaced the normal form. Jesus Himself commanded us to go and make disciples, and then to baptize them in Matthew 28:19. The order of the actions is very clear – commitment to Jesus Christ must come before the water of baptism.)

One of the biggest problems is that people baptized in this newer and non-Biblical form were baptized into a denomination or church, but not into the Kingdom of God. This is a vital difference not widely recognized, but it does need correcting to fulfil the clear instructions of Jesus Christ.

In nations like India, where the Kingdom of God is growing at an exponential rate, those who lead people to Christ have the express duty and responsibility to baptize those converted, and then to do the follow-up discipleship, where they train the new converts to do

the same. This is the original New Testament model and is a major factor why God's kingdom is growing there so fast.

An Interesting Account

Before we summarize this topic, let me provide a true and compelling account. A family from England went to live in Thailand for the father's employment. Just along the road from their house was a Buddhist monastery. The children sometimes visited the monastery. One of the boys decided after some time to become a Buddhist monk, and learned what that required. He was good at what he did, and in his later teens was invited to return to England to help establish a Buddhist centre there. He did this, but his family, who were nominal Anglicans, remained working and living in Thailand.

After some months in England, this young man met up with some real Christians, and had many discussions with them about matters of faith. After reflection, this young man decided to become a follower of Jesus Christ, and so he abandoned Buddhism. After making a decision to follow Jesus Christ, he was discipled about what that meant. Part of this included instruction on Biblical baptism. He decided he should do this, and did so.

Some months later, circumstances allowed him to return to visit his family in Thailand. After a few days with his family, he decided to go to the monastery and visit his old friends, the monks who lived there. As he walked into the monastery several monks he had known met him. They looked very shocked to see him. When they recovered from their shock, one told him that they knew he had died and could not explain how he now appeared to them alive. The young man asked when his death had supposedly occurred. They had been keeping him in their prayers, until a particular date when they sensed he had died. He assured them that he was actually alive, and had not died. But the date they named was not his conversion to Christ, but the date of his baptism. For reasons only God can explain, the day and time of his baptism was exactly when the monks lost him in the spiritual realm. While I have no explanation for this event, it does indicate significance in our spiritual journey when we obey Jesus Christ's command to repent, believe and be baptized.

In Summary

* Baptism is a command for all believers in Jesus Christ. It is not optional.

* Baptism in water is taking a public stand with God and righteousness against the devil and sin.

* Baptism is a challenge to the powers of darkness. It says, ***"Now I am living for the Lord Jesus!"***

* Baptism is an act of faith calling on the grace of God for strength to overcome in all things with which we struggle.

* If Jesus needed to be baptized then we also need to. (His need was to provide an example to follow in obedience and surrender. Jesus' baptism was a sign of the empowerment of the Holy Spirit, of authority and the commencement of His ministry.)

Excessive ritual is unnecessary. However two questions should be asked of anyone who is requesting baptism. These are:

1. ***Do you confess with your mouth that Jesus Christ is Lord, and believe in your heart that God raised Him from the dead?***

2. ***Do you come willingly to be baptized, in obedience to the command of the Lord Jesus Christ?***

When these are both answered in the affirmative, the time and place of the baptism may then be arranged, whether formal baptismal pool in a church building, a river, the sea or a home pool.

Let all Christians obey God in these important issues so that Jesus Christ would be glorified through His Body – the people of God!

"Then Peter said to them, "Repent, and let everyone of you be baptized in the name of Jesus Christ for the remission of sins; and you shall receive the gift of the Holy Spirit... Then those who gladly received his word were baptized; and that day about three thousand souls were added to them." (Acts 2:38, 41).

Appendix Three

HOW TO REVERSE THE CURSE ON YOUR WEALTH

This teaching is not about the money - it's about proving God's Word true. Let us look at some definitions first.

Money: a current medium of exchange in the form of coins and bank notes
ORIGIN Middle English: from Old French *moneie*, from Latin *moneta* 'mint, money,' originally a title of the goddess Juno, in whose temple in Rome money was minted.

Poverty: the state of being extremely poor:
• the state of being inferior in quality or insufficient in amount:
• the renunciation of the right to individual ownership of property as part of a religious vow.
ORIGIN Middle English: from Old French *poverte*, from Latin *paupertas*, from pauper, 'poor.'

Prosperity: the state of being prosperous:
ORIGIN Middle English: from Old French *prosperite*, from Latin *prosperitas*, from prosperus, 'doing well.'

Wealth: an abundance of valuable possessions or money well-being; prosperity.
ORIGIN: Middle English *welthe*, from well or weal, on the pattern of health

The Background

In John 10:10b Jesus said,
"I am come that they might have life, and that they might have it more abundantly."

Did Jesus succeed? If the answer is "yes," why do people still not have the more abundant life? I have heard many involved reasons

for why people do not have the more abundant life. It may have to do with fear, unbelief, ignorance, disobedience - all those things, but the root of the cause lies in the first part of John 10:10, “The thief comes not, but for to steal, and to kill, and to destroy.” (The devil is the thief.)

In what could be called “Prehistory” when Lucifer was expelled by heaven, God saw a way of training mankind by allowing Lucifer to have influence on the Earth. Lucifer caused Adam and Eve to doubt God’s words and promises, so their survival on Earth now required hard work.

Later on, God chose Moses to lead His people out of slavery in Egypt. We all know the story in Exodus, partly covered in the origins of The Passover. When the people of Israel prepared to depart Egypt, Moses told his people to ask their neighbors for their gold, silver, clothing and other wealth. While they couldn’t eat those things, and God promised to supply food and water for them all, the people of Israel were owed four hundred years of back-pay. (See Exodus 3:22, 11:2). In Biblical types, Pharoah was a type of the devil.

It’s interesting the Exodus should have taken eleven days of walking to the land God had promised. However, because of their stubbornness and disobedience, it took forty years. That generation died in the wilderness until God raised up another generation to replace them. *(I note it’s a bit over forty years since the “Charismatic Renewal” burst upon churches almost globally. That generation is also dying off because they didn’t fulfil God’s requirements and most seemed to stay with religion through denominations, instead of His Kingdom focus.)* Even Moses was prevented from entering the Promised Land, due to his disobedience, so leadership passed to Joshua.

“The angel of the Lord smote Pharaoh and spoiled him. He will do it for us just as he did it for the children of Israel. He makes a distinction between the children of God and the children of the world. The angel of the Lord fought for God’s people, took the wealth, gave it to the children of Israel and they walked away with the wealth that was their pay.” (“Devil, Give Me Back My Money” by Dr. Dale Sides.)

"Moses was not the only warrior who spoiled the devil. How about King David? Do you know why Israel rose to the prominence that they did under David's leadership? David was a man after God's own heart. He was a warrior!" ("Devil, Give Me Back My Money" by Dr. Dale Sides.)

"And David took the shields of gold that had belonged to the servants of Hadadezer, and brought them to Jerusalem." 2 Samuel 8:7

"David knew the rule of warfare, "To the victor go the spoils." Every time they beat a country, they went in and took all their gold. Well, every time Israel got beat up, the devil took it from them. The Philistines took the Ark of the Covenant out of the tabernacle, too. Verse 11 talks about all the things which David brought back with him:

"King David dedicated these to the LORD, along with the silver and gold that he had dedicated from all the nations which he had subdued " 2 Samuel 8:11

"Subdued" means "conquered." This is what Adam was supposed to do, to subdue the world. This is what Moses and David did, and what you must do. "To the victor go the spoils."" ("Devil, Give Me Back My Money" by Dr. Dale Sides.)

The Angels

Angels are ministering spirits that minister for you - to make your enemies your footstool (Hebrews 1:13–14). In the spiritual realm they excel in strength (Psalms 103:20) and they encamp round about you (Psalm 34:7) to guard your perimeter and to advance your position against the enemy. They play a major role in getting your wealth and treasure back from the devil; they are the warriors and couriers.

They are heavenly spirits ministering for you in spiritual warfare. The results of their wrestling in the spirit realm are manifested in the physical realm.

"But to which of the angels has He ever said: "Sit at My right hand, Till I make Your enemies Your footstool"? Hebrews 1:13

This is talking about spiritual warfare. Notice that making your "enemies your footstool" is set in the context of the angels. About these angels, the next verse says,

"Are they not all ministering spirits sent forth to minister for those who will inherit salvation?" Hebrews 1:14

Angels minister for you. They are ministering spirits sent to minister for you. They ministered to Jesus in the wilderness, in Matthew 4:11. And they will minister to you.

Please note that angels - ministering spirits - are not for us to command. They can only receive orders from God Himself. So, we ask God the Father for our needs to be met, as the Holy Spirit guides us, and in the name and authority of Jesus - Yeshua Ha Mashiach.

In Daniel chapter 10, Daniel prayed and fasted until a messenger or angel got to him. (Just as well he didn't stop on day 20.) Do we need to fast and pray for twenty-one days before the result is obvious? No, it's not a prototype or pattern because every circumstance will be different. The issue is that your attitude is right in line with God's will, as well as your faithfulness.

If your need is material wealth (as opposed to spiritual change) when it begins to arrive you will need to be very careful you don't get greedy. That's the spirit of Balaam (Revelation 2:14). That's a spirit of bribery that can buy your allegiance and commitment, just like Balaam tried in Numbers chapter 22.

As wealth arrives, be generous, support ministries that have good fruit and faithfulness for God's Kingdom.

"Do not lay up for yourselves treasures on earth, where moth and rust destroy and where thieves break in and steal; "but lay up for yourselves treasures in heaven, where neither moth nor rust destroys and where thieves do not break in and steal. "For where your treasure is, there your heart will be also. Matthew 6:19–21

When dealing with money, tithing quells the spirit of Balaam. The spirit of Balaam tries to kill a church or ministry through starvation, like Jezebel does through manipulation and control. The spirit of Balaam says, *"Tithing is not in the New Testament."* But it's in the book of Hebrews, and that is in the New Testament. It also says, *"I can't afford to tithe."* Statements like these are a sure manifestation of that demon. For those who say, *"Well, I am not under the law of tithing," I say, "That's fine, don't be under the law of prosperity, either. They both work together, hand in hand."*

Would you mind paying a tenth if you had seven times more money than you do now? Most folks would say, *"Oh yes, we would be glad to give a tenth, then."* Angels minister for those who are about Kingdom business. Start paying at least your tithe now. Nevertheless, the Lord wants you to be prosperous. Look at the men of God in the Old Testament. Look at a few of God's wealthy men: Job, Abraham, David, and Solomon. There was nothing wrong with them being wealthy. That was, in fact, God's provision for them.

Get your vision focussed and properly aligned in the will of God. For God's sake, for Jesus Christ's sake, and for the ministry's sake, we need to win people for the Lord Jesus Christ. Evangelism and discipleship should be happening in every church fellowship that claims to be Christian. If these are not happening, we should question if they are genuine Christians. That's what our need is - and why we need all of our money. Develop the right perspective of wealth. Use it to build the Kingdom of God. By God's mercy and blessing, be wealthy. Be prosperous. Be generous. Be obedient. Pay your tithe. Remember, you can't take it with you, but you can "wire it ahead."

How to Proclaim

If you have the authority Scripture says you have, then find out the Holy Spirit's will, and proclaim it.

Be specific!!!

Dr. Derek Prince writes there are two related words: **Confession & Proclamation**

Confession means we say the same with our mouth as God has already said in His Word. Our words agree with God's Word. **"Jesus is the High Priest of our confession." (Hebrews 3:1)**

Proclamation is confession made aggressive: It is a word of spiritual warfare. It is releasing God's word into a situation in our lives, the life of the church or ministry, or whatever.

Dr. Derek Prince writes: *"Over the past three years Ruth and I have been fighting a continuing war against Satan, who has opposed us and our ministry in many different ways. His primary goal has been to kill Ruth.*
In this war the Holy Spirit has taught us how to take the Bible as our rod and extend God's authority through it into every area where Satan has been opposing us.

The Holy Spirit has led us systematically to Scripture after Scripture, and has shown us how to direct them to each area where Satan has been opposing us.

The strategy which the Holy Spirit has taught us is:

Proclaim!

Thank!

Praise!

First, Proclaim the appropriate Scripture with bold unwavering confidence.

To make this fully effective, we often personalize the passage we quote, making any grammatical changes needed to apply it personally to ourselves.

The second step is to accept the Scripture we have proclaimed as true, even before we see its actual outworking in any situation. The natural result of this is to thank God for it.
This leads logically to the third step: loud jubilant Praise." ("Prayers and Proclamations", Dr. Derek Prince, Introduction)

Proclamation Examples:

“And they overcame him by the blood of the Lamb and by the word of their testimony, and they did not love their lives to the death.” Revelations 12:11

(Then personalized)
“And I overcame him by the blood of the Lamb and by the word of my testimony, and I do not love my life to the death.”

“I shall not die, but live, And declare the works of the LORD.
The LORD has chastened me severely, But He has not given me over to death.
Open to me the gates of righteousness; I will go through them, And I will praise the LORD.
This is the gate of the LORD, Through which the righteous shall enter.
I will praise You, For You have answered me, And have become my salvation.” (Psalm 118:17-21)

“No weapon formed against you shall prosper, and every tongue which rises against you in judgment you shall condemn. This is the heritage of the servants of the LORD, and their righteousness is from Me,” says the LORD.”(Isaiah 54:17)

A Sample personalised Proclamation:

“No weapon that is formed against me shall prosper, and every tongue which rises against me in judgment I do condemn.

If there are those who have been speaking against me, or seeking harm or evil to me, or who have rejected me, I forgive them (name if known).

Having forgiven them, I bless them in the name of the Lord.

Now, I do declare Oh Lord, that You and You alone are my God, and besides You there is no other – a just God and a Savior, the Father, the Son and the Spirit – and I worship you!
I submit myself afresh to You today in unreserved obedience. Having submitted to You, Lord, I do as Your word directs: I

resist the devil and all his works, all his pressures, his attacks, his deceptions, and every instrument or agent he would seek to use against me. I do not submit to him but resist, drive and exclude him from me in the name of the Lord Jesus Christ

Specifically, I reject and repel all infirmity, pain, infection, inflammation, malignancies, allergies, viruses, every form of witchcraft and every type of stress.

Finally, Lord, I thank You that through the sacrifice of Jesus on the cross, I have passed out from under the curse and entered the blessing of Abraham, whom You blessed in all things: exaltation, health, reproductiveness, prosperity, victory, God's favor and God's friendship." (quoted in "Winning the Spiritual battle in the Courts of Heaven", Selwyn R. Stevens, Ph.D., pps 55-58)

Have those who have taught you God's Word included teaching like this? If not, it's time they did. If they won't teach you this, then ask Holy Spirit to lead you to people who will.

First, get your attitude right with God and others. Remember how much the devil and his agents has stolen from you and remember that when a thief is discovered he must restore seven times over (Proverbs 6:30–31). Be angry and sin not. Do not give place to the devil (Ephesians 4:26-27), and get your rightful place of authority back from him.

Next, ask Father God to send the ministering spirits out to collect and return what the devil and his agents have stolen from you! And after you do it, when the money comes, don't forget to pay your tithe.

Stay faithful. Do you know how much money God wants you to have? All that belongs to you! And when you get all of it back, don't forget why you have it: It is to supply God's Kingdom with what it needs to advance His Kingdom everywhere.

We all need money. Maybe that God's calling for you is to make money to support effective ministries. There is plenty to go around.

Hallelujah! Be obedient. Be faithful. Be thankful. Do this faithfully! As I was completing this teaching, I was sent the following by a friend. It was written by Fiorella Giordano:

"Wealth is more than finances, wealth is a force. The word for wealth used in Deuteronomy 8:18 and Isaiah 60:5 is the word 'Hayil' pronounced 'Chayil', which means valour, force, host, army, influence.

Wealth is a manifestation of dominion.

The wealth transfer is not a financial exchange only, finances are simply a manifestation of it, but rather it is a transfer of forces and it is a generation or regeneration of forces, when heaven gives you power to create wealth, it gives you power to create a force to guide the rivers of its influence with might and strategy.

May you be filled with valor that is being fuelled by a divine system of abundance, may everything that you put your hand to be graced with the majesty and power of a heavenly army, may it shine with the radiance of the host of heaven, may your ideas unseat the governance of carnal wisdom and grace the earth with the majesty of the wisdom of God. May you be established in the reigning force of the wealth and abundance of God so that the blessing of God established ages and your genealogy."

"Then you will see and be radiant, And your heart will thrill and rejoice; Because the abundance of the sea will be turned to you, The wealth of the nations will come to you." (Isaiah 60:5)

"But you shall remember the Lord your God, for it is He who is giving you power to make wealth, that He may confirm His covenant which He swore to your fathers, as it is this day." (Deuteronomy 8:18)

What does God's Word say about all this?

"The earth is the LORD'S and the fullness thereof," Psalm 24:1.

“Beloved, I pray that you may prosper in all things and be in health, just as your soul prospers.” 3 John 2

“And my God shall supply all your need according to His riches in glory by Christ Jesus.” Philippians 4:19

“Do not lay up for yourselves treasures on earth, where moth and rust destroy and where thieves break in and steal; but lay up for yourselves treasures in heaven, where neither moth nor rust destroys and where thieves do not break in and steal. For where your treasure is, there your heart will be also.”Matthew 6:19–21

“The thief comes not, but for to steal, and to kill, and to destroy: I am come that they might have life, and that they might have it more abundantly.” John 10:10

“Blessed be the God and Father of our Lord Jesus Christ, who has blessed us with all spiritual blessings in heavenly places in Christ.” Ephesians 1:3,

“Honor the LORD with your possessions, and with the first-fruits of all your increase; so your barns will be filled with plenty, and your vats will overflow with new wine.” Proverbs 3:9, 10

“He who tills his land will be satisfied with bread, but he who follows frivolity is devoid of understanding.” Proverbs 12:11

“He delivers the poor in their affliction, and opens their ears in oppression. Indeed He would have brought you out of dire distress, into a broad place where there is no restraint; and what is set on your table would be full of richness.” Job 36:15 -16

“Oh, fear the LORD, you His saints! There is no want to those who fear Him. The young lions lack and suffer hunger; But those who seek the LORD shall not lack any good thing.” Psalms 34:9 -10

“Delight yourself also in the LORD, And He shall give you the desires of your heart. Commit your way to the LORD, Trust also in Him, And He shall bring it to pass.” Psalms 37:4-5

"I have been young, and now am old; Yet I have not seen the righteous forsaken, nor his descendants begging bread. He is ever merciful, and lends; And his descendants are blessed." Psalms 37:25-26

"He shall regard the prayer of the destitute, And shall not despise their prayer. This will be written for the generation to come, That a people yet to be created may praise the LORD." Psalms 102:17-18

"That I may cause those who love me to inherit wealth, that I may fill their treasuries." Proverbs 8:21

"Lazy hands make a man poor, but diligent hands bring wealth. He who gathers crops in summer is a wise son, but he who sleeps during harvest is a disgraceful son." Proverbs 10:4 (NIV)

"But seek first his kingdom and his righteousness, and all these things will be given to you as well." Matthew 6:33

"Be anxious for nothing, but in everything by prayer and supplication, with thanksgiving, let your requests be made known to God." Philippians 4:6

"But if they do not listen, they will perish by the sword and die without knowledge." Job 36:11 (NIV)

"If they obey and serve him, they will spend the rest of their days in prosperity and their years in contentment. "This Book of the Law shall not depart from your mouth, but you shall meditate in it day and night, that you may observe to do according to all that is written in it. For then you will make your way prosperous, and then you will have good success." Joshua 1:8

"If you are willing and obedient, you shall eat the good of the land;but if you refuse and rebel, you shall be devoured by the sword; for the mouth of the LORD has spoken." Isaiah 1:19-20

"Let them shout for joy and be glad, Who favor my righteous cause; And let them say continually, "Let the LORD be

magnified, Who has pleasure in the prosperity of His servant."" Psalms 35:27

"And my God shall supply all your need according to His riches in glory by Christ Jesus." Philippians 4:19

"Pray for the peace of Jerusalem: "May they prosper who love you. Peace be within your walls, Prosperity within your palaces."" Psalms 122:6-7

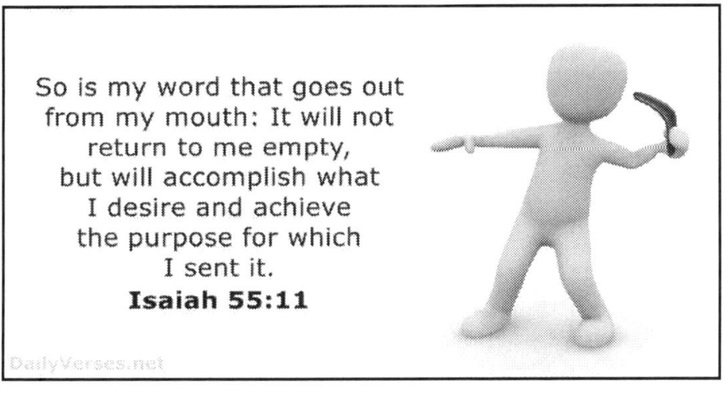

God didn't decide to love anyone. But God IS love, without exceptions. God never created anyone unloveable. Jesus gave us the divine exchange from Satan's disorder to God's order. Too many have believed the lie that this life is as good as it gets, when we are wallowing in circumstances of lack, or poverty.

Many examples of this are found in the Word of God. Jesus, our great example, said: **"Peace, be still,"** in Mark 4:39; **"Stretch forth your hand,"** in Matthew 12:13; and **"Lazarus, come forth,"** in John 11:43.

This is the way you proclaim your health and wealth back from the devil.

"Are they not all ministering spirits sent forth to minister for those who will inherit salvation?" Hebrews 1:14

"Bless the Lord, you His angels, who excel in strength, who do His word, heeding the voice of his word." Psalm 103:20

I want to come back to this Scripture: **"And my God shall supply all your need according to His riches in glory by Christ Jesus." Philippians 4:19**

Does God lie to us?

No! He can't, He says so in His Word in Psalm 33:4.

So when He promises to supply all your needs, but should you have a lack, then someone or something has stolen it from you, and it wasn't God.

It's time to do something effective:

Here's a sample prayer of Proclamation you might use:

Because it is God's intent through Jesus Christ - Messiah Yeshua - that all principalities and powers should know the manifold wisdom of God through His Ecclesia (according to Ephesians 3:9-11);

And because the True, Holy Creator God wishes that I may prosper and be in health, even as my soul prospers (according to 3 John 2);

And because My God shall supply all my needs according to His riches in glory by Christ Jesus, (according to Philippians 4:19),

And Lord God, I choose to seek first Your kingdom and Your righteousness, (according to Matthew 6:33);

I belong to God through Jesus Christ - Messiah Yeshua, and what He did for me on the cross at Calvary. He entrusted me with stewardship of health, relationships, money, possessions and property, some of which you, devil, have stolen;

So, having already been supplied with all that I need, whatever has been stolen from me by you, devil, or your agents, according

to Proverbs 6:30-31, you are now required to restore to me seven times what you have taken;

So, I now proclaim and declare to you, devil, in the name of Jesus Christ - Messiah Yeshua, that you must now restore to me all my health, relationships, money, possessions and property, with the seven-fold restitution that God has declared in His written word;

Living Father God, I am not asking you for any of this, because you have already given them to me. I do ask, though, for You to dispatch ministering spirits to go and get these and bring them back to me, that I may restore my stewardship to the glory of Your Son, Jesus Christ - Messiah Yeshua;

For surely, Oh Lord You bless the righteous, and You surround them with your favor, as with a shield, according to Psalm 5:12.

Praise the Lord Most High!

The Blessing, May God:
Remember you like Noah
Favour you like Moses
Honour you like Mary
Fight for you like the Israelites
Prosper you like Isaac
Promote you like Joseph
Intervene for you like Esther
Protect you like Daniel
Use you like Paul
Educate you like Timothy
Heal you like Naaman
Answer you like Elijah
Anoint you like David
and Keep you safe like Shadrach, Meschach & Abednego.

About the Author:
Selwyn R. Stevens,

Ph.D; D.Min.; M.I.S.D.M.; M.E.A.C.M.

is the President of Jubilee Resources International Inc. a New Zealand-based educational and religious organization involved in informing and equipping Christians of all denominations how to reach the lost and deceived in cults, the occult and secret societies such as Freemasonry. Author of over 35 books (and co-author of two), including twelve Best Sellers, an International Speaker (on five continents) and ordained minister. Dr. Stevens is a third-generation preacher, and has been involved in various Christian groups, and also maintains an active interest in national and world affairs and politics. Dr. Stevens is a Foundation Member of the International Society of Deliverance Ministers, founded by Dr. C. Peter Wagner and convened by Dr. William & Sylvie Sudduth of Texas, USA; and Apostolic Overseer of the Alliance of African Christian Churches & Ministries based in Zambia. Regular Facebook and e-mail teaching and mentoring is also provided to many Christian leaders across Africa, Asia & Latin America, resulting in tens of thousands being equipped for service to the Kingdom of God.

About Jubilee Resources International

God's commission for Jubilee Resources International is based on Ezekiel 33:1-9, and Luke 4:18-21. According to the Bible, Jubilee years were times of restitution. Debts were cancelled, slaves set free, families reunited and lost or forfeited inheritances restored. Every year was prophetic of the ministry of Jesus Christ. The Jubilee was proclaimed on the basis of the work of the High Priest on the Day of Atonement - so Jesus Christ's liberating ministry is founded on His atoning work. Jesus began His public ministry by reading the passage from the prophet Isaiah (Luke 4:18-21). All the liberties of the Jubilee year are now available to us through the redemptive work of Jesus Christ at Calvary, and we all have the responsibility to preach this Gospel of Redemption and Restoration to full Relationship with Yahweh/Father God. When Yeshua/Jesus Christ returns, God's people will be totally free from all sin, sickness and disease, death and curse. The Biblical Jubilee will then be fully realized.

Resources in print book, eBook, audio & video formats are available in English, with paper & eBooks in Spanish, German, French, Italian, Portuguese-Brazil, Polish, Ukrainian, Russian, Dutch, Swedish, Danish, Norwegian, Finnish, Hungarian, Romanian, Slovak, Czech, Greek, Bulgarian, Estonian, Latvian, Lithuanian, Afrikaans, Malaysian, Indonesian & Tagalog, with other languages pending.

Additional Resources Available by Selwyn R. Stevens, Ph.D.

www.jubileeresources.org (Webshop)

Plus comprehensive range of free tracts to download

Raising a Blessed Generation. The goals of this teaching are three-fold:
Goal 1: To understand what Blessing is and the Power it has for our lives today;
Goal 2: To Identify and Recover any missed blessings in my own life;
Goal 3: To Begin to Learn How to Bless others, especially our children & grandchildren! Identity and gender confusion is caused by the failure of parents & grandparents to speak identity and destiny into the young ones. Best Seller *Book, E-book, MP4 video*

How to Recognize the Voice of God. How does God communicate to His people? How will you know when it is Him speaking to you? This very practical teaching has already helped many. *Book & MP4 video*

Daniel and the Star Chasers. The counterfeit of Astrology has hidden what God wanted His people to know about the Gospel message in the stars. Daniel taught that truth to the Magi of Asia, and that nearly caused the War of the Continents half a millennium later. Only in recent decades has mankind had the technology to uncover what the Magi saw. Following Daniel's instructions, they went to see the King of Kings and submit their kingdoms and empires to His. *Book, E-book, MP4 video*

The Christian Life & the Role of the Fivefold Ministry. The Christian church is being increasingly side-lined in social debate. Have we ceased to be the Salt and Light commanded by Jesus Christ? The Solution: become real Christians! But what does that entail? Then, how are Christians to be governed? God provided the Fivefold ministry to do that. What does that look like? Best Seller *Book, E-book, MP4 video*

Help! The Sheep are Escaping: Understanding the Exodus From Church to God's Ecclesia. For most Christians in the West, "church" isn't working! The Old Wineskin cannot compete any longer, as God raises up His New Wineskin to fulfil His end-time purposes. The solution is for "church" to become Ecclesia and for participation with appropriate equipping, releasing and accountability.*Book, E-book, MP4 video*

Biblical Healing Training Manual. This thorough examination of Biblical physical healing is the result of many years of experience as well as training under some of the world's best Bible teachers. There are many "How To's", practical prayer and ministry guidelines, reasons why some aren't healed, and what we can do about them, etc. Hundreds have been healed, & many congregations have been empowered to commence regular Healing services with Christ-glorifying results. Best Seller *Book, E-book, MP4 video*

Dealing with Curses & Generational Iniquities. This teaching offers hope for all Christians that they can be released into the blessings of God and forever leave behind iniquities and curses that have kept them captive, perhaps their whole families for generations. This explains the twelve major curses that people may have operating in their families, and what to do about them. It also includes new material on the curses over Scottish, English, Irish, Welsh and Scandinavian people, plus many other national and ethnic groups. This teaching has been taught in several nations with much fruit for personal, family and community liberty. Best Seller *Book, E-book, MP4 video*

Dealing with Demons: *Insights into evil spiritual influences.* This popular teaching provides outstanding insights regarding evil spiritual influences that exist in the world in which we live today, and then goes further to show us what to do about it. Best Seller *Book, E-book, MP4 video*

Insights into Martial Arts, Tai Ch'i TM & Yoga. Much of the western world has seen an explosion of these practices. For many, their involvement has became close to a religion, adopting belief systems, mind sets and practises inconsistent with the teachings of the Bible. Best Seller *Book, E-book, MP4 video*

Treated or Tricked - Alternative Health Therapies Diagnosed. Many people are now trying Alternative Health Therapies. This book explains the various medical & spiritual healing methods; investigates whether the "Energy/Life Force" is scientific or spiritual; and describes almost 80 different Alternative Therapies, from Aromatherapy to Zone therapies. Also examines reasons why some are not healed & how to overcome these failures Biblically. Co-authored with Dr. Badu Bediako, (former Assoc. Professor of BioChemistry.) Best Seller *Book, E-book, MP4 video*

Unmasking the Adventist Paradox: Foundations of Delusion. Is the Seventh-Day Adventist church just a Christian denomination that is a bit legalistic about the Sabbath and dietary issues, but otherwise a "Christian" denomination? This book will help you understand the times in which it began in the 1800s, and how those affected the thinking of many people at that time. Out of the failed prophecy by William Miller about the Return of Jesus Christ, there arose a variety of new religious movements, many of whom borrowed each other's dogma.

The Seventh-day Adventist Church was one of those movements, picking up a mixture of delusions that are still largely held by their members. This is a group founded by a proven false teacher and false prophet, Ellen G. White, whose errors and visions have become dogma. There is always a danger when dogma becomes legalism, when they take the traditions of a man or woman and elevate them above the Word of God.

Like the Roman Catholic Church, which the Seventh-day Adventists criticize a lot, both are in desperate need of Biblical correction if they are to be regarded as legitimate branches of Christianity. The Paradox is explained in Matthew 7:15-20, Galatians 3:1-3 and James 3:11-12. *Book, E-book,*

Unmasking Freemasonry - Removing the Hoodwink. Written primarily for the wives & families of Masons to explain the curses brought on themselves and their families through the oaths; then learn how to deal with the effects. History & structure are explained simply. A Past Master who read this book immediately resigned from his Lodge. The prayer guidelines from this book are being used by many ministries worldwide. 7th edition with endorsement by C. Peter Wagner. Best Seller *Book, E-book, MP4 video*

Unmasking Mormonism - Who are the Latter-day Saints? Learn about LDS founder Joseph Smith on whose credentials this cult fails Bible tests, the Book of Mormon hoax, Mormon polytheism, true & false priesthood & authority. This book has caused many Mormons to cancel their baptisms & leave to seek the genuine Jesus Christ - the One from the Bible. Best Seller *Book, E-book, MP4 video*

Unmasking the Watchtower - Who are the Jehovah's Witnesses? This asks the questions many J.W.'s are being expelled for daring to ask! Check out the changeable prophecies and man-made doctrines of the Watchtower, the authoritarian leaders & their use of Mind-Control & manipulation of members, how to know the One True God, and how you can witness to and pray for a J.W. effectively. Best Seller *Book, E-book, MP4 video*

Discerning the Past to See the End Times: *Islam's Role in the Return of Jesus*. The statue in Nebuchadnezzar's dream, interpreted by Daniel, gives us a clear picture of the various empires that have sought domination of the Middle East and beyond. World events circle around this area of vital interest to God and His people. The Bible is a Middle Eastern book, not a European or American book. The context of the empires of the statue give us vital clues about the Empire of the Beast to come! Best Seller *Book, E-book, MP4 video*

Rome's Anathemas: Insights into the Papal Pantheon. This vital book investigates Constantine's divorce of the Jewish roots of the Christian faith and its replacement with paganism; the Council of Trent rejected the Biblical basis of Luther's Reformation and cursed all who disagreed with them. In John, we read of the marriage feast at Cana. Realizing that the wine was gone and that she herself could not do anything, Mary tells Jesus, because He is the only One who could do something. Mary then gives the stewards her last recorded words and only command - one that we must consider for us to be saved. Mary said, *"Whatever He say to you, do it!" Book, E-book, MP4 video*

Signs & Symbols: Cult, New Age & Occult Insignias & What They Mean. From Ananda Marga, Anarchy, & Ankhs, to Yin & Yang, Yoga & Zodiacs. By popular demand this book has a brief explanation & a Biblical comparison with dozens of insignias. 8th Edition, Best Seller *Book, E-book*

Fatal Faith - the Cult Counterfeit of Christianity. This book explains how cults develop and what patterns to avoid. Key Christian and Cult beliefs are compared with the main active cults. How to handle door-knockers, cult exiting, pre-cult spiritually-abusive churches; and how to protect young people from cults. Major ancient & modern heresies examined. Best Seller. *Book, E-book*

The New Age - the Old Lie in a New Package. New Age & Bible beliefs and practices compared, including Reincarnation and Past lives, Astrology, the New Age pseudo Messiah, Self-worship & our Deity-potential. Energy/ Life Forces are examined, and the occult involvement of most holistic health gurus. Best Seller *Book, E-book*

The Bible 101. A teaching manual introducing the Bible, explaining clearly it's purposes, origins, history, inspiration, symbolism, translations & versions, moving from milk to meat, study helps, rules of interpretation, and how to study it to get the best understanding. *Book, E-book, & MP4 video*

Additional Resources Available by Selwyn R. Stevens, Ph. D.

www.jubileeresources.org (Webshop)

Plus comprehensive range of free tracts to download

Made in the USA
Columbia, SC
10 September 2024